... FOR SNOW

A Caribbean-Canadian Chronicle

SAND FOR SNOW

A Caribbean-Canadian Chronicle

Robert Edison Sandiford

LIVRES
DC
BOOKS

Sand for Snow © 2003 by Robert Edison Sandiford

DC Books 950 Decarie, Box 662   Montreal, Quebec H4L 4V9

Editor for the Press: Steve Luxton.
Cover design and layout by Geof Isherwood.
Book designed and typeset by *Sasigraphix* in 10-pt Sabon.
Printed in Canada by AGMV Marquis.

Canada Council   Conseil des Arts
for the Arts   du Canada

DC Books acknowledges the support of the Canada Council
for the Arts and SODEC for our publishing program.

0-919688-79-9 paperback   0-919688-81-0 bound

Dépôt légal, Bibliothèque Nationale du Québec and The National Library of Canada, third trimester, 2003.

First Printing.

National Library of Canada Cataloguing in Publication

Sandiford, Robert Edison, 1968-
      Sand for snow : a Caribbean-Canadian chronicle / Robert Edison Sandiford.

ISBN 0-919688-81-0 (bound).—ISBN 0-919688-79-9 (pbk.)

      1. Sandiford, Robert Edison, 1968-. 2. Authors, Canadian (English)—Barbados—Biography. 3. Black Canadians—Barbados—Biography. I. Title.

PS8587.A368Z53 2003   C818'.5403   C2003-906664-9

For Sherry, who brought me this far,
and Dad, who put me on the path.

Acknowledgements

I would like to thank Harold Hoyte of the *Nation* news-paper in Barbados, Egbert Gaye of *Montreal Community Contact,* Odette Dixon Neath of *SkyWritings*, Air Jamaica's in-flight magazine, and my publisher Steve Luxton for joining me on this carnival ride.

'Home' is a place where one feels a welcome.

—Caryl Phillips, *The Nature of Blood*

Preface

Two things took me to Barbados in the spring of 1996. Not the sea and sun, as some might imagine, rather my wife-to-be and work. I was to be married in Montreal in December of that year to a Barbadian, and journalism opportunities were increasingly limited to me in a city with only one major English-language newspaper. It was time to explore my options. The island of my parents' birth seemed a good starting point.

I had pitched a column to both Barbadian dailies in March 1995 — the *Nation* responded favourably. I was commissioned to write a weekly one on North American-Caribbean issues, as I had proposed. I continued to write it, among other articles, when I joined the staff as associate literary editor, from May 6, 1996, to December 13, 1999.

The column was called The Onlooker. I was 28 and conscious of not setting myself at too great a vantage point from my readers. That was not at all what I wanted, being a Canadian of Barbadian descent. A cousin of mine once said to me, "It's the onlooker who sees most of the game." Coming from a Barbadian who immigrated to Canada in the '60s, the observation stuck.

I was also aware of the challenge I had embraced. It was doubtful — despite talent, connections, hype, or friendship — that I would have been so fortunate to land such a space in Montreal, Quebec, Canada, permitted to write every week in 500 words, more or less, about the things that mattered to me most: like my brand of Canadianness, life in Barbados, literature and writing, the spirit of my age, doing the right thing (whatever that was), friends and family.

Sand for Snow: A Caribbean-Canadian Chronicle owes much to these reflections, rants, enquiries, entertainments, and outright digs, including other articles, profiles and travelogues written for international publications while based in Barbados. It is indeed a chronicle — a record of events as they struck me, hard — drawn from this very deliberate, sometimes desperate spilling of words.

Coming out of the Caribbean as they did, and just at the turn of the millennium, these stories could not have been written in any other time or place. Yet I recognize, too, that they were very much the product of an identifiably, a stubbornly, North-American state of mind, equal parts exultant and distressed.

For that recognition — and appreciation — I am most grateful.

RES, January 24, 2003

SAND FOR SNOW

A Caribbean-Canadian Chronicle

1996

Love — it makes the world go 'round

THE QUESTION I'm most asked by Barbadians when I tell them I've moved from Montreal to this island is "But do you like it here?"

This enquiry, I've been informed, is inevitable. In the opinion of a friend of mine who moved from England to Canada six years ago, natives always want to know how immigrants find their country.

Since no country is perfect, they're somewhat surprised somebody would want to assume the responsibilities of another place. It's as if they're really saying: "Don't you have enough problems of your own?"

To answer both questions at once, I have come to appreciate Barbados in many respects. I'm not just talking about the sea, the sand, or the stars at night. I've never been one for holiday pictures of things only. A people make a place for me.

Barbadians are a tough-talking, heavy-politicking, sunny-looking kind of people. They often remind me of my fellow Canadians. We have our disagreements, but we can all get along.

And Barbados certainly has its share of ills. A lingering class system from the British, a disaffected youth, a high incidence of HIV/AIDS infection for its size, and the constant threat of American incursion into its affairs, to name a few. But my duty as a citizen will be to help preserve what is good in this country while doing my best to improve what is not.

As a Canadian-Barbadian (my parents were born, raised, and married here before leaving for Canada in the late '50s), this move will be a challenge, physically, mentally, culturally, socially, and, of course, financially. Setting up home and shop will not be easy.

Still, whoever said money makes the world go 'round was wrong. It's not the almighty dollar that's got me on the go but Love with a capital "L." I'm moving to Barbados because the woman I love is here.

I've known for a long time there are options available to me in Barbados that could benefit me and my work. Yet I would never have explored them as fully as I have nor as soon if not for falling in love with The Mrs.

There is no place I'd rather be than with her. For the foreseeable future, that means primarily in Barbados.

Who says love — real love — between a man and a woman is dead? A married, middle-aged Bajan man once confided in me: "Love between a man and woman now seems to be a thing of the past, you know. They really don't seem to love anymore." But I beg to differ. I've known too many men and women — friends, family, and acquaintances — who have been moved in all sorts of powerful ways by the ones they love, in the name of love.

What is love?

"Love is patient and kind," says the Bible; "it is not jealous or conceited or proud; love is not ill-tempered or selfish or irritable. Love never gives up and its faith, hope, and patience never fail. Love is eternal."

And Coleridge once said: "Love is a desire of the whole being to be united to some thing, or some being, felt necessary to its completeness."

I say love is passionate, feeling and strong, among many other wonderful things. Yet without risk, pain, or sacrifice love would not be what it is: the principle by which we judge all actions, the emotion on which we rely simply to survive each passing day.

The Mrs means much to me. We make each other happy. I know peace of mind when we are together and unrest when we are apart.

We've had good times and bad times, yet I have never been more confident in my ability to weather the highs and lows of a relationship.

She turns me on—with her lithe body, her soft voice, the startling thought of her.

Actually, my wants become indistinguishable from my needs when I think of her.

The Mrs is that much a part of my life. We are that committed to each other.

Now I realize there are those — many, perhaps — who will not, cannot, understand this reasoning or these feelings any more than they will or can understand why I would move from a country like Canada, with all the conveniences, to a country like Barbados, still coming into its own. Unbelievable, they say. More foolish than romantic, more impetuous than pragmatic.

But I like it in Barbados just fine, thank you. I am with the woman I love and wish to be part of the scene.

And to quote Shakespeare — should I require any further defense — "If this is error, and upon me prov'd/ I never writ, nor no man ever lov'd."

May 6

Speightstown revisited:
looking for my father

I WALKED the streets of Speightstown the other day looking for my father. I had been feeling homesick and longed
for some connection with the familiar. Speightstown is
where Dad grew up, a place he and his brothers often
spoke of, mythically, when I was growing up. It was the
world of his "boy days."

Dad was what people used to call a supremely capable man: he trained as a teacher and organist in Barbados,
immigrated to Canada in 1958, brought over his wife, a
nurse, a year later, obtained his BA and MA from Sir
George Williams University and McGill University, respectively, was a globe-trotter and well-read, an amateur
botanist, a faithful husband, a committed family man.

This isn't to say Dad didn't have his limitations.

Among them was his inability to see writing, my
avowed vocation, as more than "a hobby." Having a
"profession," to Dad, was being a doctor or a lawyer or a
rocket scientist. It was not being a writer, much less an
artist. I don't even think it was being a teacher or a nurse.
He wanted to be a doctor or a lawyer when young, and
would've been, but his old man couldn't afford it.

To me, a profession is something you do to make a living and by which you can partially define yourself. Dad, a
very ambitious West Indian and from a much different
school of thought, believed otherwise.

But there has been a great absence in my life since Dad
became ill with Alzheimer's over 10 years ago. For all our
disagreement, I miss the benefit of his counsel. Dad was a

man of considerable empathy and wisdom. (He still is, actually. The sharper your edges, the harder it is for the disease to dull you.) He always took the time to explain things: tennis, himself, right from wrong, volcanic rock formations (his subject was Geography). "Dialoguing," he used to call it. That was the teacher in him.

At the same time, his absence has forced me to be my own man relatively early in life.

Anyway, Speightstown's not so bad on a Saturday night.

It struck me as a smaller version of Bridgetown: fairly busy, fun, a little scary around certain corners. I only knew what it might be like from what Dad and his brothers had recounted during family get-togethers, from what I had read in travel guides, and from drive-bys (not even drive-throughs) on visits to Barbados in previous years.

I walked along the bright beach the way I would along the shores of the Saint Lawrence River in Montreal, stirring with emotion, lost in thought. It was a place where Dad might have swum far, far out with his brothers, heedless that the sea has no backdoor. Then I wandered the sandy streets I imagined Dad used to run, the way he must have on restless nights, dreaming a life for himself in another country.

I kept looking for him as if he were a ghost or spy, but I did not find him. When I couldn't locate old Speightstown Boys' School, which he had pointed out to me in 1986 — when I realized the building that had housed it might be gone — I stopped looking.

It has been almost 40 years since Dad was in Speightstown. I would not find much of him there or, for that matter, anywhere else on the island. The most important parts of him are now found only in the memories of myself and others.

Although it would be good to think those memories will sustain me forever, there have been those times I have sat with my father, simply holding his hand in mine, and cried at the loss of him, this man who once led groups of people on summer treks through Mexico, and across Canada and the US, but who can no longer find his way home.

He led by example; he was that kind of strong, proud, black West Indian man. What kind of example was I to follow now, when even my own memories can shift like sand?

I do my best to be philosophical. Every journey has a destination, even if unanticipated, and that destination could be the discovery of the self as much as that of another. My trip to Speightstown was hardly a waste.

After so many years of making the island's acquaintance, I'm going to have to find out what Barbados is all about on my own terms. I'm going to have to make new memories, like friends, to rely on to bring me home when home seems so far away.

June 3

Thoughts on being Bajan

TODAY, I AM a Barbadian.

Almost a year ago, I began the process of claiming my Barbadian citizenship. Since my parents are natives of Barbados, I was entitled to it by descent. Last month, in one of my Mom's weekly CARE packages, I received the four-line notice granting me my request, along with my certificate of citizenship from the Chief Immigration Officer.

My first feelings were slow but sure: I was pleased, thrilled even, at finally being recognized as Barbadian.

I have been a Canadian my entire life so, in a sense, have not had to think hard about what this means to me. As much as I believe nationality and, to a certain extent, culture are accidents of birth, a Canadian — a *Canuck* — is what I am.

(And *not* an American. Too many people in Barbados take the liberty of making this mistake simply because it's supposedly easy to make. Whereas Americans talk about the Melting Pot and their dream of a just society, Canadians talk about the Mosaic and their ideal of a harmonious community of communities. Whereas Canadians have been shaped by their landscape, Americans, by and large, have tried to shape theirs.)

Of course, I've made a conscious decision to be a Barbadian and this carries with it a couple of considerations.

The first is the question of what it means to be a Barbadian. The other is the understanding that, despite the citizenship, I will never be truly Bajan.

Maybe I should give myself more time. A Barbadian

for a whole two months, I'm already (it seems) predicting the nature of my life here.

As a Canadian, though, I get a little frustrated when I look out to open sea. There's something reassuring about being backed by plenty of land, and Barbados is smaller than Montreal — I don't even have to compare it to Canada, the second largest country in the world.

I also feel this frustration — and The Mrs suffers it — when I'm driving. Sixty km/h is a comfortable speed to me. Yet The Mrs is forever reminding me to "slow down, please."

She trusts my driving — I take it she wouldn't buckle up with me if she didn't, and we're talking on the left side of the road here — but sometimes, honestly, I can see her eyes closing and her body bracing when we lean into a curve.

My points of reference are also different. You say "boot," I say "trunk." You say, "It's common sense, when turning around using a side street, to reverse boot first then pull out with your bonnet facing the road." I say, "What the hell difference does it make as long as you watch for oncoming traffic?"

And then you look at me as if I'm mad. I've gotten into some remarkable misunderstandings with Barbadians claiming to be keepers of 'common sense.' But as a college friend of mine has observed: "Common sense is usually neither — kind of like the Moral Majority in the United States." Put another way, Bajan common sense is not necessarily Canuck common sense and vice versa.

If I sound ambivalent about my new status, I guess I can't help it. After a lifetime of being raised by Bajans, you'd think I'd be more of a natural at being one. But a sense of difference persists. Even if, as the saying goes, "the onlooker sees most of the game".

This isn't to say I have any regrets. Why should I pretend to be something I'm not? If I'm going to be praised or damned, let it be for who and what I am.

Some days, I am a man happily caught between two countries. Other days, I am a man searching for a place to call rightly my own.

Today, I am a Canadian who is proud to be called a Barbadian, too.

June 10

Piece of paradise gained?

FROM A DISTANCE, the valley looks hazy. Whether rain or shine, you see it as if through smoke-filled eyes, as if by magic. Green and brown, rich and fertile, pastoral, idyllic.

I call it a valley. That's what it seems to my sensibilities, this stretch of land below Yorkshire Development in Christ Church. The wind gently blows the young canes and trees. Majestic clouds drift overhead, forming white lions and horses. The valley lies cradled between bright, low hills dotted with cream-coloured houses.

A piece of paradise is what many would call the valley, Barbados, presumably, being the whole. 'Beautiful Barbados.' 'Island in the Sun.' With the country's recent third-place ranking in readiness for the North American Free Trade Agreement, Barbados would appear to deserve the status.

But the honour is dubious — even if this is how Barbados has been viewed or has come to prefer to be viewed.

It's pleasant enough to be considered a paradise. Except the one great advantage — unconditional affection — is outweighed by one great disadvantage — sentimental misconception.

Not a few of my friends in Montreal called me a "lucky dog" for moving to Barbados. They saw me sipping rum punches as I typed on the beach. They saw me kicking around coconuts like story ideas. They saw me partaking of remarkably inspiring, sea-spawned vistas. If only they could see me now, penning this piece in a cramped, sweaty space, much as I worked in Montreal.

Actually, Canada also received a third-place ranking

from the United States-based Institute for International Economics. Like Barbados, yet in its own way, "Canada whispers to us all," as Laura Williamson sweetly put it in the May 6 issue of *Maclean's*, Canada's weekly news-magazine:

> You can hear "Canada, Canada" when you sit in a grove of cedars on Vancouver Island and watch the whales playing offshore. You can sense Canada in the foothills of Alberta, with the purple mountains hovering in the distance. You can smell Canada in the coloured fields of Saskatchewan and Manitoba; the lonesome call of a loon on Lake Winnipeg inspires a feeling of solitude and a kind of arching Canadian melancholy.

> When the leaves are changing colour in Ontario, the glassy lakes reflect such vivid beauty one has to pause and meditate.... Can one walk along the banks of the mighty St. Lawrence and not feel awed by its power? One sees the sea reflected in the eyes of Maritimers. The mysterious North — can anyone watch the Northern Lights and not hear the whispers?

Williamson's description is so pure and true, you'd think Canada was a paradise. You'd think the grass really is greener there, not merely a little less trodden. But Canada is no more a paradise than Barbados. Descriptions such as these, though moving, never paint the full picture.

After all, if Barbados were a paradise, there would be no hurricane season. If Canada were a paradise, it wouldn't get so damn cold in winter.

This isn't to say Barbados isn't some kind of tropical wonder. Don't get me wrong. This is just to say it is a country distinguished by more than beautiful scenery and brilliant sunshine, and, in my estimation, all the better for that.

June 17

Looking forward to Crop Over

I GOT MY first taste of carnival in Montreal. Not in Barbados, as you might expect, nor in Trinidad, Land of Carnival. Being born in Montreal had something to do with it, but *Carifête,* the city's Caribbean carnival, was as much a part of growing up there in summer as learning to skate at the park in winter.

There was a time *Carifête* was *the* Caribbean carnival in North America. People journeyed from the United States, England and even the Caribbean the first Saturday in July to take part. The sweet strains of soca and calypso infected everybody.

Bands of merry men took to the streets, and children begged to play *mas'* — dress in costume and go on parade. The women cooked up a storm of peas and rice, beef stew, fried chicken, roti.

The last *Carifête* I vividly recall took my Mom, Dad, my little sister, and me down to Man and His World, the site of Expo '67. Some of the pavilions were still in good shape, so it must have been during the late '70s, early '80s.

The day was sunny, hot, but we walked all the way from Montreal, where the parade began, to Ile Ste-Hélène, across the Jacques-Cartier Bridge, where it ended on the old fairground. My sister held my Mom's hand, I held Dad's. It felt like we would walk forever; it felt like we could.

And the number of people! It was a day to meet family and friends you only counted on meeting once a year, at carnival — if you could spot them in the crowd.

For the parade wound up in a mass of swaying bodies and smiling faces with flashes of purple and red, and green and gold, wherever we looked: huge pin-wheels and pea-cock feathers, glorious crowns and fierce standards, brilliant robes and trains whose majesty was worthy of African kings and queens. Just like during Crop Over, Barbados' annual jump up.

These are the great memories thousands of others and I have of *Carifête* (many proud Torontonians included. When Toronto's Caribana was still fighting for its survival — in desperate need of guidance, money and respect — Montreal's Jump Up, first marched in 1973, a year before Crop Over's revival, was already massive. It was the carnival that, in the words of a 1986 Montreal *Gazette* headline, "put[s] out the welcome mat.").

Carifête has had its ups and downs and a name change to Carifiesta. And Caribana, today, is the Caribbean carnival in North America everybody talks about, can't miss, celebrates, remembers. Yet this tradition of carnivals is one of the most remarkable Caribbean transplants.

This tradition is also something for which I am thankful. It would be some time before I saw a Crop Over in Barbados. But watching its offshoot parade down the streets of Montreal helped teach me about calypso's contribution to world music and literature, about the value of community efforts and about having pride in my heritage.

Each year, critics of Crop Over ask what the young get out of it. They want to know, for instance, how a massive street party benefits them. For an answer, they might ask my parents, who view carnival as a reality of their lives as West Indians.

Gatherings of six or more loud people can be disturbing to Dad now, and my Mom is always fearful of losing him in a crowd, no matter how tightly she holds his hand.

Still, they jump. My parents believe — and have passed on this belief to their children — that they are no less respectable or learned because they can shake a leg (or other parts of their bodies), and like a good time.

To them, life, pop-music commentary aside, is neither a highway nor a party, but an adventure, a challenge and, most of all, multi-faceted.

According to a report prepared for the National Cultural Foundation, Barbados is expected to gross a healthy $30 million in foreign exchange from Crop Over this year.

In this way, Crop Over has become valuable to Barbados. But there are other reasons carnival has its place here and elsewhere.

July 8

Poor-man's parliament

A SHOP IN Barbados is a place of power. Most notable is the well-stocked shop, which offers more than the sum of the items on its shelves.

A well-stocked shop in Barbados has character and charm, craft and cunning. It teems with human activity — economic, cultural, social, sexual — and never sleeps.

The shopkeeper's business, traditionally, is that of the people: his (or her) people, other people's people, all the people who would come to him and purchase his goods.

It matters little what the sign above his door says he sells. The customer is always first and knows what he (or she) wants anyway; that is to say, a bit of human exchange, personal interaction, and the benefit of counsel from a gathering of one's peers.

So people come and go, talking shop. They gossip, reminisce, tender opinions.

They talk about the weather and the season and how God continues to renew His Bajan passport. Either that, or Barbados is one of His preferred vacation spots. Another year, and no hurricane can touch us.

But if God is truly a Bajan, why aren't His people more gracious? That's what one woman wants to know: "I go to the market and ask this person nicely how much such and such is. And do you know what this person tell me? 'De *same* as it was yeste'day.'"

The woman is indignant. Someone mutters: "So unmannerly." Another says: "It doesn't cost a body one red cent to say, 'Please,' 'Thank you,' 'You're welcome,' or even simply to smile."

There are nods all around.

The conversation moves on to a survey of "the latest": the latest fashions and, consequently, walking embarrassments, the latest movies at The Globe (drive-in or cinema) and pirated video releases, the latest, unforgettable crimes and the anguished prayers they elicit for swift, sure justice, if not revenge.

Talk slips from the hangman's noose back to God: "Barbados is the closest country to God," says the shopkeeper. "You can't get 'way with anything here." There are more nods all around.

The mood changes. The day progresses.

By noon, people are talking about lunch, where they'll eat and what. They trade clever ways to stretch a half-hour break into one, one into two, without their bosses' knowledge or retribution.

In the afternoon, they wind down. Belly full, tail drunk, they begin to reflect on their day's labour, on what they have done and what they have left undone. They consider how much they have profited from what they said and heard.

And somewhere, in a far corner of the shop, as the sun goes down, coral-coloured dominoes flash hard against a table, slammed by a heavy hand. A man calls for another cold one then for something to eat.

He folds his arms and looks from face-to-face, listening. Amid the laughter and cheer of drinks, he waits for the next round.

September 30

Home for the Holidays

THE LIGHTS ARE up as if for a show, the decorations in the mall are well-worn but familiar. Snow falls, feather light, dusting everything. Once again, 'tis the season in Montreal.

With talk of parties and presents, family gatherings and last-minute shopping, the Christmas spirit has been generated. Some would say mass-produced. Christmas is a brilliant time for manufacturers as much as for children-of-all-ages here.

But it is good to be home for the Holidays. In recent years, Christmas has become a period of reflection for me. I've done some of my most satisfying thinking while walking along the Saint Lawrence, its flow frozen now, wandering like a man without a country, which is how I increasingly have come to view myself since moving to Barbados, like a hapless *agent provocateur*.

Why is it, no matter how far a Bajan may roam — to study, to work, to live — he or she will always look to Barbados as a place to return to?

What is it — nostalgia, myth, fond memories — that holds captive the restless imagination and enquiring heart in that inescapable prison known as 'Back Home'?

Ironically, the toughest Bajans I know have been or are abroad. Yet they are also the most sentimental.

A sense of displacement is unsettling regardless where you come from or where you're headed. It's like feeling forever out of synch with the world around you.

There's always a deep need: to return to the familiar, the safe, the sure, even if time and circumstance change everything, leaving nothing tomorrow as it was yesterday — quite possibly making the safe risky, the sure uncertain, and the familiar strange indeed.

The Mrs and I have come home to be with Dad, not knowing if I'll see him again before he loses another piece of himself, or drifts away altogether. As long as he's alive, I'll be coming back home, to Montreal and to him.

"That's Robert. Rob," my Mom repeats in a practiced voice. She has spoken these words to him in exactly the same way a hundred times in my absence, prompting that famous teacher's memory of his.

His mouth opens mechanically, his tongue twists. "Rob-Rob," he says, one of his first endearments for me. And possibly his last. These are hardly Christmas thoughts, warm and reassuring. They are, however, thoughts for the season here in Montreal, where the Quebec government seems determined to enforce the politics of exclusion, where all I can think of is how to keep a life whole, memories intact.

Their oppressive language policies — which attempt to dictate who can speak either English or French, where and when — continue to pit the French against the English, the indigenous against the immigrant. *Je me souviens*? What? Anything important?

I am reminded of the words the British writer Alan Moore wrote in 1988 shortly before quitting England for the US:

"I'm thinking of taking my family and getting out of this country soon, sometime over the next couple of years. It's cold and it's mean-spirited and I don't like it anymore."

These aren't the reasons I left Montreal — I went to Barbados in search of opportunity, work, love — but they are why I would stay away. No matter how many long walks along the Saint Lawrence I take, I can't romanticize this place as I once did.

But even if coming back home as I wish is out of the question, Montreal, Quebec, Canada, remains my home. I can't demonize it. Nor am I prepared to give it up.

Home: we all have one, all go back to it, if only in our minds: as a place from which we were formed, where we hope always to feel a welcome, a sense of belonging, and where the heart beats strongest.

December 23

1997

The folly of Valentine's Day

S HE GETS up, goes to the window. It's a windy, sunny day. I lie in bed, awake, wondering what she'll do when she's done greeting the sun.

It's late, maybe 7, 7:15. We both should be up by now: me, to do some writing, she, to do housework. But we don't get many opportunities to retreat from the world — probably because you've got to take them — they aren't given you.

I'm pleased when she closes the window instead of saying, "You ready for breakfast?"

I know couples who take time out once a week, usually on a Friday, around the dinner table, to talk to each other about their hopes and fears. And I also know couples whose bathrooms and cars double as private chat rooms: they fill each other in on their lives as they shower for work, bring each other up to speed on their way home from the office.

For The Mrs and me, two avid nappers, our talk is pillow-talk. We often examine our lives together from the vantage point of our bedroom.

We discuss where we might go for Valentine's Day dinner Friday. A buffet on the west coast sounds appealing. With the recent introduction of VAT, it seems more prudent than ever to choose a restaurant that offers quantity eats as well as quality service.

We remind each other of upcoming anniversaries: the anniversary of our marriage, the anniversary of my proposal and her acceptance, the anniversary of our first kiss.

We share our dreams and plans for the next 75 years.

And these include more studies and work, a few children, travels throughout Europe and the Caribbean — even who will most likely take care of whom in old age, which we tell ourselves is anyone's guess.

The past is remembered, too: in uneasy reflections on former friends and lovers. But the past has long since been put in perspective; it's the future we focus on. We laugh, embrace, kiss.

When The Mrs and I were married in Quebec, we were struck by the nature of the agreement we were about to enter into as laid out by the province and the Anglican Church of Canada.

It was an agreement as binding as any we had ever signed with a bank or insurance company. In our minds, it was clear: this business of marriage was just that.

And for this business to thrive we would have to develop a heightened sense of responsibility, honour and openness toward each other.

This remains our response to the marriage contract. We don't pretend to know how other couples come to terms with it.

It is the hubris of every young couple in love or every couple newly in love to wonder if any two individuals have ever been as close as they. The joining of two hearts, two minds, two bodies, and two souls is one of the most powerful, profound, and personal acts known to man and woman.

Still, marriage is not a wholly natural state, and love is indeed highly overrated. Marriage is largely a social construct, and love is worthless if not backed up by commitment.

The notion of two, unique human animals living in harmony for the rest of their lives is slightly absurd. It defies logic. Even the Bajan priest who prepared The Mrs and me for marriage was not embarrassed to confess this.

Yet the folly of Valentine's Day, a day dedicated to the unselfconscious profession of love, attests to the fact neither love nor marriage is about perfect sense. Emotions are what we respect, not gifts of gold, chocolate or lace. The more sincere the emotions, the more worthy they are of respect.

As so many long-married, long-loving couples have observed, it takes challenge, desire, instinct, and risk to keep the honeymoon sweet. It takes constant effort to turn a youthful passion into an eternal flame.

February 10

Savouring the art of ease

THERE AREN'T ENOUGH days simply to do nothing. There aren't enough days unrestricted by the home, unstructured around the workplace.

I enjoy my job, and I love my family. Yet there are times I could do with fewer demands and a more flexible schedule.

Like George (Jason Alexander) on the television sit-com *Seinfeld*, who wanted to write a show for NBC "about nothing," I appreciate the allure of inertia, the art of ease. I'm wise to the benefits of chilling, of doing that which relaxes us by requiring no more effort on our part than what we are willing to expend.

It has been said that Bajans work too hard, and there is a degree of truth in the statement. There aren't enough days for many to do even the obvious, like go to the beach, bathe till you shrivel like sea moss, then lie on the sand, dry off in the sun, have a picnic afterward.

There aren't enough days to look out the window without having anywhere in particular to go, days to fix those tiles in the bathroom down the hall, to rid the garden for good of weeds or wash the living room curtains — days to do those things you've been wanting to do but just haven't been getting around to, like writing a letter or listening to some music or viewing tape after tape from the video shop.

No, there aren't enough days to take long, lazy naps or long, roving walks, depending on your mood, days when the choice of activity is yours entirely.

You can sit quietly with a loved one, settle an old disagreement. Or you can sit alone on the dusty verandah to see the sun rise above smoky clouds, wondering little other than what kind of day it will be: how hot, how windy, how rainy.

You can lie in bed all day with a book, pausing as you please to luxuriate in the drama, the mystery, the adventure of the words. Or you can go back out on that verandah with that same loved one with whom you've finally made peace and split a fat, green and yellow mango, its golden juices spilling from your chins, your fingers a sticky, sweetness.

Besides money, time is all we ever really seem to desire more of.

Time to visit relatives or a sick friend, to talk, eat, drink, laugh, and reminisce into the early hours of the morning, when the stars come out and bright clouds rush the moon, and everybody's feeling drowsy and mellow.

Time to spend without watching the clock, without always having to be some place else five minutes ago.

Time to travel, try a new recipe, take a muscle-massaging bath instead of a wake-up shower. Time to listen to a stranger, a spouse, a child...and respond, because we can, having stopped long enough to hear what was being said to us.

Call this a lament. Call it wishful thinking. I'm simply calling it as I see it. Doing nothing isn't necessarily doing nothing at all.

March 3

Going the whole hog

IT USED TO be a tradition, in the days before I moved here: when my parents and I visited Barbados, about every three years or so, this old-time friend would call us up and ask us out to lunch.

He never took "No" for an answer, and he never took us to the same place twice. He almost always took us to a hotel's restaurant, and we almost always had the buffet.

Thinking back, the only thing surprising about those culinary excursions is that I was never disappointed in them.

I've managed to carry on a version of this tradition. The Mrs and I have a couple of buffets we look forward to frequenting whenever we're back in Montreal.

The Mandarin is a popular Chinese restaurant. They serve the expected — egg rolls, frog's legs, chicken chow mein — and the unexpected — French fries, pizza, Jell-o.

The second, Vichy, is what you might call a 'scoff and trough.' Breakfast, lunch and dinner are served simultaneously: golden pancakes, French toast and omelets, barbecued chicken, fried rice and diced potatoes, roast ham, pork, lamb, turkey, and endless mounds of salads and fresh fruit.

For approximately $10 per person (tax included), it's simply outrageous. And the Mandarin, being more specialized, charges about $5 more per person for its fare, which is still a great deal.

Cheap, American-style buffets are not common, however, in Barbados. Being true food lovers, this is something The Mrs and I miss: the all-you-can-eat eatery, where you can go back for as much of whatever you like as often as you like for a few bucks.

I know of one instance only in which two people were barred from a buffet. They are friends of my brothers', bear-like men, who could devour stacks of lasagna and roast beef in one sitting. Their appetites so scared a proprietor one afternoon that after their third trip he was telling them they had had enough already.

Since then, both men live more moderately. One had a heart attack, which resulted in a healthy change in lifestyle, the other went on a crash diet after he and his partner broke up, slimming down quite handsomely.

But I find my passion for buffets undiminished.

The best thing about these buffets is the variety they present to the food amateur and connoisseur alike, whether the offering is modest or lavish.

I try not to overindulge. I'm not for gluttony or waste. Too much of any good thing can spoil the pleasure. Although I've seen people eat nothing but platefuls of sticky-sweet spare ribs or buttery grilled shrimp kebabs.

The Mrs herself consumes practically nothing but the vegetables at the Mandarin, our preferred buffet. "Forget the meat," she says. The crunchy, sauced broccoli-and-cauliflower combos are what she spoons heavily onto her plate.

I have a favourite aunt who used to talk of returning to Barbados to retire. She dreamt of pushing around a little hot-dog cart to keep her busy and in a bit of pocket money.

My aunt was a nurse; she retired recently. She hasn't mentioned this dream in a while. I don't even know if she still has hopes of coming Back Home.

But if her dream is alive, I'd encourage her to change it a little. OK — a lot. For The Mrs and me.

"Think buffet," I'd tell her. "American-style." Why go for a single wiener when you can have the whole hog?

May 26

Bajan man-talk

I'VE NEVER CONNECTED fully with the sweet-talking, sex-driven, saga-boy image of Bajan men. My father, Bajan-born-and-bred, is a good man. His brothers, also of The Rock, are good men.

By this I mean they are strong, hard-working, caring, intelligent, reliable, gentle men capable of showing love, faith, and fidelity. By this I mean my image of Bajan men has been, for the longest while, positive.

I've known worthless Bajan men, been acquainted with the type through work, social gatherings and gossip. But I believe all people are individuals first. All people have their excesses. Some, more than others.

I often look to Dad and his brothers and other men of honour to understand better the type of man I should be, the type of husband and father. These men also have their vices: they are personal heroes, not gods. But I never felt their weaknesses would ever jeopardize my well-being.

I wonder who boys and young men in Barbados — my little brother-in-law, my wife's good friend from church — look to for instruction in an environment where male role models seem to be at a premium.

After finally living in the island, I've become keenly aware of my heritage as a Canadian-Barbadian of African descent. I am all these things at once, yes, yet in this specific order. My influences are more than Caribbean but primarily North American.

Moreover, my father, although by all accounts a serious young man well before he left Barbados for Canada, was undoubtedly changed by his exposure to new perspectives on and experiences of manhood in his adopted country.

I came of age in the 1970s and '80s, during a time when women were talking about wanting men to be more sensitive, domestic, sharing.

Many of my close, boyhood friends, cool guys (they aspired to be, in any case), had younger sisters. So did I. But all of us, growing up, were the ones who cleaned the house on weekends, who could really cook, wash, sew, iron, who had little difficulty empathizing with people, especially small children.

We were still directed to fulfill the 'traditional' expectations our parents couldn't help but have for us, being boys: to find solutions, take the lead, build the nation. The new, additional expectations didn't replace them. Given the pressures of socialization, how could they? But these cool guys and I are today, as young men finding our way in the world, more skilled for having had to meet them.

Somehow, I doubt my male, Bajan contemporaries have had the same experience.

The greatest problems facing Bajan men are no different than those facing men elsewhere. They confuse being macho with being manly, talk with action, ability with responsibility, anger with passion, overconfidence with strength. It could be just taking them a little longer to realize this, admit it to themselves, and do something about it.

I think my point is, as strange as it may sound, that there has to be the recognition that men are just as capable as women, that they not only can be honest, intimate, and understanding but that they are, or strive to be.

June 11

Springtime in Barbados

IT'S ALMOST A mood thing, this shifting awareness of nature.

The awareness comes suddenly, like a scent, a whiff of something freshly baked and sweet.

It comes while standing at the window looking at low clouds or riding the ZR home an evening or lying in bed under a fan, cooling off, the wind rustling the leaves of the trees, heat and sunshine everywhere. And it is strange, like déjà vu.

It's hard to pinpoint what occasions these sensations. It could be schoolchildren running across a crossing, a walk in the park, the colour of the sky on a particular day.... I may be wrong, but I imagine it's hard for people who have never experienced the four seasons — winter, spring, summer, fall — to appreciate them fully: the rhythms and reassurances they provide from age to age, their feasts, festivals, and celebrations, the startling change in scenery, not just in weather.

Canadian winters can be cold, yes. But years after learning in grade school, while cutting out paper snowflakes, that each snowflake that falls from the sky is different, I'm still thrilled by their delicate, singular beauty.

It's little wonder the Inuit have dozens of names for snow. There are so many ways to understand it: through snowmobiling, skiing, skating, building a snowman, even snowball-fighting.

Then there's the comfort of hot chocolate, warm blankets, woollen sweaters, and fireplace chats.

You might think winter's my favourite season. It's not. Autumn — fall — is.

Temperate is the best way to describe it, in terms of the weather, yet passionate, too, with the changing of the colour of the leaves from green to yellow to purple to red.

It's back-to-school time, but it's also time for thanksgiving and All Hallow's Eve and the solemn remembrance of those who lost their lives in war. The air has a crispness, and people move with a briskness.

The problem with summer in Montreal, which is where I'm thinking of, is that it can get oppressively humid besides hot. 'Muggy' is the word. And it's easier, to me, to warm up than to cool off.

But I enjoy the lakeside picnics and the late-night talks by open doors and 9 p.m. hikes up Mount Royal by the light of a setting sun.

And to think the reason for all this yearning and musing is spring, my least favourite season, which is almost over now, and a desire to see the thawing of the land of my birth, the emerging of people from their wintry grey gloom.

I hate the dampness, the aggravation of allergies, and the seemingly endless waiting for the world to be reborn. But I miss the bursting of the tree buds, the tilling of the soil, and the sowing of the seeds of promise.

June 16

Curiosity and the cat

THERE ARE CERTAIN things I have no desire to know.

I don't want to know when the world will come to an end. I don't want to know the circumstances of my own demise. And I don't want to know a surprise if it is meant to be a surprise.

Then there are those things I wouldn't mind knowing.

I want to know hope truly exists. I want to know life has meaning. I want to know how people find their way and place in an ever changing world.

Although this last isn't the type of curiosity that breeds gossip or malice, it makes my days less dull, more interesting.

This particular ZR conductor, for instance, asks The Mrs for her umbrella. "Don't mean to be rude or disrespectful, dear, but can I borrow that?"

It's raining again, and he's out hustling (some would say "hassling") passengers into the van. "This way, love birds, this way," he says, whether you look like a happy couple or not, whether you're alone or in a group.

He's quick and good-natured and can hold his own.

The terminal's a mess: oily pools of water banked by trash, vans clustered. A traffic jam soon forms at the usual exit.

There are no policemen to keep the flow of traffic orderly. The drivers cuss and threaten each other.

"I've had it with you ZR men!" says one ZR man.

Our conductor begs another for a pass. "C'mon, man, give me a break."

Taking his time, the ZR man complies.

Our conductor is ragged and wet. He has got to be

tired, too. Yet what makes him so enthusiastic, so sure he can move the world, defy the elements? Neither love of work nor money seems to account for his temperament.

The woman in the bank reminds me of my publisher. She's lanky to lean, tends to duck her head as she speaks and moves with an endearing awkwardness.

She's not your usual teller; she sits at one of the customer service desks. Her shy smile makes me appreciate her helpfulness all the more.

She wears no wedding ring. And you can tell plenty about a thirty-something-year-old Bajan woman from her marital status. I pretty much can see how she spends her days Monday to Friday, 8 a.m. to 3 p.m..

She likes what she does. She prides herself on being able to meet her customers' needs.

But how does she spend her nights, her weekends? Who is she outside the confines of her desk? What about her life beyond the bank's wired doors? She looks like a bright person, a person who likes to laugh and make others laugh.

There are those who say, "Curiosity kills the cat." Sometimes, it does. Careful what you seek to know — you may be shocked at what you find out.

I believe curiosity can fatten. There are those who also say that: what doesn't kill fattens. And curiosity can be quite filling.

July 7

Puerto Rico: Listening to Charlie Zaa

SO HERE WE were, The Mrs and I, sitting in the middle of the Rio Piedras, an outdoor mall in San Juan, Puerto Rico, sharing a soft vanilla ice cream in a sugar cone and listening to the sounds of a Latin pop singer with the unlikely name of Charlie Zaa.

We had spent too many hours cruising the shops along the street and were looking for a place to cool off before heading back to our pick-up point. The sun was hot, and The Mrs chose a spot by a music store.

In the store's window was a TV playing music videos of Zaa's songs. Above us hung a poster of Zaa.

The poster was a blow-up of his album cover. A head shot, it showed the singer in black and white, slightly hunched over and looking off to the side, with a scarf around his neck covering the lapels of his tuxedo.

With his dark hair and daring looks, Zaa was reminiscent of Frank Sinatra in his prime. In fact, the whole album, entitled *Sentimientos*, was evocative of the big-band era.

The more I watched the videos, which were also shot in black and white, the more I admired their quality. And the more I paid attention to the rhythm of the words and the melody of the music, the more I liked their playfulness and passion.

By the time The Mrs was ready to leave, I was humming Zaa's songs, mouthing the lyrics, and ready to buy *Sentimientos*. And I was somewhat surprised at myself.

The least of my concerns was not speaking Spanish — I didn't own a Walkman or stereo, either.

I used to commit such acts of spontaneity all the time in Montreal — still do when I'm there visiting the homestead.

But I realized I tend to feel — or, more accurately, am made to feel — a bit weird for acting on impulse in Barbados.

Regardless how beneficial or pleasant the act, such behaviour is often perceived as subversive here. A lack of choice or funds can further hinder a person's ability to be wild and crazy in the best sense imaginable socially.

Truth is, though, that in a society where there is great pressure for people to conform it's difficult to be dynamic — to follow your instincts, follow your heart. The status quo is supposedly the way to go. Not even reason wins out.

What brought on the desire to purchase Zaa's album — besides the classy packaging and infectious music — was simply the atmosphere.

It wasn't that I felt 'less inhibited' as a tourist or that I was inspired by stereotypical notions of how 'free-spirited' Latin Americans are.

I appreciated the right to be just another face in the crowd, remarkable, perhaps, because of who I am, not because of what I appear to be; unique, yes, yet neither more nor less noteworthy because of the colour of my skin, the brand of jeans I wear, or the way I walk.

Just another guy sharing an ice cream with his wife and listening to Charlie Zaa on a busy street, trying to take in the various sights.

August 18

The breadfruit and the maple leaf

THESE ARE the good days.

I wake up before the sun. Put on my sweats, an old, holey T-shirt and a blue-jeans cap. Long socks and running shoes. A glass or two of water, then I'm out the door.

It's Saturday. I pull on my grass-stained gloves. Although it doesn't deter me — I hardly notice 'til the work is done — my hands blister easily.

I start by chopping the wild cane that grows from the property next door onto our yard. The machete is rusty dull. I hack away like a man with murderous intent.

I'm building up a sweat. But there's something liberating in the release of force it takes to cut the cane. Pile the stocks for garbage.

I roll out the lawnmower. Fill 'er up with gas. Set the speed (between the tortoise and the hare) and pull the cord. I'm off.

The grass is tall, thick and dewy. I drag the lawnmower back and forth. I watch for frogs and centipedes.

The frogs usually leap out of the way when they hear me coming, but the thought of mowing over one makes me superstitious. Centipedes, I consider cousins to scorpions. Nuff said.

A couple of branches of our coconut tree are heavy. I call out to The Mrs; she's up washing down the counter tops in the kitchen. I'd like to take some coconuts to our neighbour, who shares his carrots and beets and seasoning with us. The Mrs reminds me of what my Mom has to get, that we promised to bring her coconut water when we go to Montreal. She says they're not ripe anyway. I never seem to be able to tell. Neither colour nor size is indicative to me. The land is different in Barbados, the soil, the mud, than that of Canada. A breadfruit tree is not a maple tree, of course. But the land is also the same. You work it. It yields. The richer it is with your blood, sweat, tears, and manure, the sweeter the bounty, the more difficult it is for the land to deny you.

I can see the sun through the leaves of the almond tree; the clouds are dissipating. Early o'clock, and it's already steamy. I sit to rest.

Dad had a green thumb. He loved plants. He kept them in his classroom at school, built himself a hot house, spent endless summer days growing okra, bonavist, plums, Macintosh apples.

When he became too ill to tend our garden, my Mom switched from being a reaper to a sower. It was an act of survival. As if keeping the garden going from season to season could help keep Dad. Or them both. He used to remind us necessity was the mother of invention.

Dad will pace our backyard while my Mom digs the earth. Sometimes, for long stretches, he'll stand beside her, staring at the grass.

I remember watering the garden for him when I was eight or nine, discussing how much sweet corn to plant with her after I moved to Barbados.

The memory makes me smile. I look around. There are still weeds to pull.

And these are the good days, the too few happy days — the days I know exactly who I am, where I'm at and why, and what I have to do to carry on.

September 1

White rebel, black cause

JUST BY LOOKING at him, you'd never guess Joel A. Freeman was the rebellious type.

Dressed as he is in blue jeans, a matching sports shirt, and brown leather loafers, he appears boyish, years younger than 43. Thin-rimmed glasses, framing studious, blue-grey eyes, add to his air of calm.

He has been the chaplain of the NBA's Washington Wizards since 1979 (he is in the island as part of the Scotiabank/Toronto Raptors' Celebrity Golf Tournament) and has worked as a pastor for almost as long. He's a family man, with a wife and four children, who makes his living as a business consultant.

When he was 17, though, he let his now thinning brown hair grow and left his parents' home in Alberta, Canada, in pursuit of "Peace. Love. Rock and Roll."

More recently, he co-authored with fellow preacher Don B. Griffin *Return to Glory:* The Powerful Stirring of the Black Man. The subtitle was his idea.

He walks fast and stoops across the short lobby. After our rendezvous, he has to check out of the Bougainvillea Beach Resort, hold a further interview, and then be in time for his afternoon flight back to the United States.

We move to the hotel's Water's Edge restaurant for breakfast. The heat is already rising from the sand on the beach.

"What we wanted to do was to have a book that would reach young black men ages 20 to 25," he explains with a soft twang. "We just wanted the message. Our names are very small at the top [of the cover]."

That message, as delivered by these two non-denominational Evangelical Christians, is that the legacy of blacks to the civilized world is beyond compare, and God has a glorious role for them as a long-suffering people.

They use the Bible as a "treasury of Black history" and scholarly texts to reveal the contributions of Blacks — from Ethiopia to the present — to the advancement of the human race. But their style is decidedly reader friendly.

"Our secondary audience is white," says Freeman. And they anticipate *Return to* Glory's appeal to women as well. "We believe that if men can be touched in a profound way, then women are happy."

Briefly, the proprietor of the hotel, a portly man with a firm grip, cuts into our conversation. Freeman rises, and so do I. He wishes Freeman a safe trip and inquires where he usually stays when in Barbados. Freeman has been to the island a half-dozen times and expresses genuine affection for the country and people, for their strength and success.

In their discussion of the effects of racism on young black men in America today — the destructive pain, anger and despair it can cause — Freeman and Griffin emphasize finding a spiritual road to "wholeness."

Seated again, he says: "It's not enough to have knowledge. It's how we apply the information."

In co-writing *Return to Glory*, Freeman was interested in "doing something" about racism.

Also the author of *God Is Not Fair: Making Sense Out of Suffering, Living with Your Conscience without Going Crazy,* and *Kingdom Zoology: Dealing with the Wolves, Serpents and Swine in Your Life,* Freeman asked nearly 50 black men about the moment they first realized their colour made a difference to others. Initially suspicious of him and his research, they eventually shared, "in vivid detail, in Technicolour," their experiences.

Freeman pauses when his breakfast is served: a sizable western omelet, wedges of cantaloupe for garnish, triangular slices of toast, and golden pineapple juice.

Before turning to his plate, he says, "We've gotten an overwhelmingly positive response…. If someone has a problem with this [book], their problem isn't with us, it's with the truth."

At least one person has told him that *Return to Glory* has defined emotions he had but could not articulate. "I think when people can name an emotion they have power over it," he says.

Freeman sees the "little ripple in the water" he and Griffin hope to stir as only a beginning of a long, inward journey.

"I think there has to be a spiritual change within the heart of each one of us," he says. "But the main theme is for mentoring young black men."

September 7

Halloween conkies

AROUND THIS SAME time last year, a majority of Barbadians were saying they had difficulty with adopting the celebration of Halloween. The number, obtained from an informal poll, was roughly 55 percent.

An even larger number of parents — 72 percent — would not let their children go trick-or-treating from house to house.

No ghosts or goblins have ever knocked on our door since I've been living here.

Halloween is considered an American thing even though Canadians also dress up for the occasion. So Barbadians' resistance to it is easy enough to understand.

In an area of the world where American influence on its affairs often can be viewed with suspicion, where national identities are yet young, hence fragile, volatile inventions, where the future of cricket and carnival as expressions of true cultural heritage is uncertain, it would seem unwise, foolish, to take on foreign traditions.

Why read "The Legend of Sleepy Hollow" to children around, say, a campfire when local legends have yet to be told around the proverbial tamarind tree?

Yet there is no reason to overstate the case.

Halloween, regardless where it is celebrated, is not about carved pumpkins lit up in windows or spirits let loose for a night. It's not about costume parties during which grown men and women bob for apples, or the conjuring of real witches.

It's mainly about giving children a few of the good things: some snacks and sweets, the chance to exercise their imaginations, memories of childhood fun that will hopefully last them a lifetime.

If there's any culture with which Halloween should be identified, it's that of charity.

Cultural appropriation can be risky business. For Halloween to mean something in Barbados, not only would a significant number of Barbadians have to get involved in it, it would have to find its own indigenous expression.

Many Barbadian-Canadians and their children associate conkies with Halloween. That ghastly pumpkin was not cut up then boiled for soup the next day or dumped on the trash heap, as were the local customs. Instead, it was grated along with coconut and sweet potato, then spiced and steamed.

The conkies were prepared in foil, not banana leaves, true, and in smaller pots than usual, but no longer on Guy Fawkes Day, as they had been for years in Barbados, when that English holiday once reigned.

October 27

She walks like a princess

CHIN UP, lips pushed out, eyes front, she walks like a princess yet with a confidence I can't fathom.

She may look damn good, but that may also be the extent of her sex appeal.

She doesn't speak, so it's hard to know what she's thinking or even if she's thinking.

And a pervasive *attitude* hides whatever she may be truly feeling.

Her beliefs, what she's really all about, are a mystery, and not the kind one is encouraged to explore.

And her aloofness makes her touch cool rather than light.

She's a type of Bajan woman (your modern Bajan woman?)

What I can't understand is why she is so humourless, why, in fact, she hardly ever smiles, yet obviously — from the walk, the short talk, the look — she feels deserving of — no, entitled to—attention or appraisal.

For as long as I can remember, I've been a sucker for a sweet smile: the kind that starts in the middle of a woman's lips and extends upward below either cheek with a flash of teeth. The richer the lips, the brighter the teeth, the more stunning the effect.

Julia Roberts comes to mind. Also Whitney Houston. And, of course, The Mrs.

It has been suggested to me that men, Bajan men in particular, have made it difficult for Bajan women to smile. They've made the women wary, cynical, at times downright cruel.

Look too pleasantly at a fellow, he might get the wrong impression and start to make an ass of himself, right? Maybe. It certainly has been known to happen, here and elsewhere. But maybe he — whoever — might just think you're happy, or you're having a good day, or you're replaying pleasant memories in your mind. You might just make the other person smile — and nothing more. The gesture has been known to be infectious.

And a smile is a gesture, not an act. I associate a smile with grace, which is giving, not wanting. It can say "welcome," "no, thanks," "let's be friends," "listen" — everything that inscrutable blank Bajan stare can't.

I'm not talking about walking around with a silly, paste-on grin. A genuine smile involves the whole face: the eyes, the nose, the cheeks, even the ears. A genuine smile can be as reassuring as looking someone in the eyes, and just as inspiring.

November 17

The Prime Minister's widow

LOOKING BACK OVER the events leading up to Barbados' independence, Carolyn Barrow insists her contribution to them was negligible.

"I think what has come out of independence is a great deal to Barbados, and to the credit of those who started independence," says the 70-plus-year-old widow of Barbados' first prime minister, Errol Walton Barrow.

She's frail, now, white-haired — being tended to in her airy, overgrown home.

"I'm busy being a grandmother."

She doesn't see what she might have to say about those changing times that would be of real value. Even though she was there: part of history, as most people are despite themselves.

Nor would she have Barbadians take their independence — their existence as a viable, recognizable, social, political and economic entity — for granted.

She quotes from Barrow's December 9, 1966, speech to the United Nations on Barbados' bid for nationhood: "We will be friends of all, satellites of none."

This is the line she would like echoed, remembered. "Two of the people who signed the United States Declaration of Independence" — Richard Henry Lee and Arthur Middleton —" were from Barbados," she says, as if to suggest the seeds of Barbados' independence had long been sown and its harvest, undeniable. She herself was born in the US.

Then she states sharply: "There's nothing about birth that is obvious.... I think the character of Barbados came out in independence."

She considers NIFCA (the National Independence Festival of Creative Arts) one of Barbados' best endeavours. Among her disappointments has been the Caribbean's failure to form a federation. She is of the opinion Barrow would have shared her sentiments.

Noting the presence of women in politics, she says: "Ah, it's been tough dragging you guys into the facts of life." But she fairly refuses to say more.

Her reticence, she claims, has made her a survivor. As a former politician's wife and Rediffusion announcer, she is ever watchful of her words — particularly in public.

"He was a terrific personality," she says of her husband, who died of a heart attack on June 1, 1987. "He had many facets; he was good at many things."

Would she call him merely the right person in the right place at the right time, or more; perhaps the Father of Independence?

"Obviously, the first person to push so," she says. "Are you leaving out Adams? He had his place." She means Sir Grantley, Barbados' first premier and the only prime minister of the short-lived West Indies Federation.

She pauses. Getting back to her husband:

"Do you think he was the father? What else would you call him? The son?"

November 30

1998

A day at the beach

HE ARRIVED AFTER midday, when the sun had begun its descent, driving a reconditioned Morris. He moved slowly, with or without the car: an older contemporary of my Mom's, one of her first cousins, which meant he was my cousin, too.

We had planned to go to the beach together for the longest while but always had difficulty setting a date. For a retiree and a freelancer, you'd think we were the busiest men on the island. Not busy, just preoccupied, he with his routine, me with mine.

I hurried out to the car and got in, my towel slung over my shoulder. He spoke the barest of greetings, a minimum of words, as if any excess of verbal communication tired him.

I gave him a nod and a "Hey, finally," and he put the car in reverse. He smiled. We understood each other. He was at that age he could say or do whatever he wanted — or not.

It took us 15 minutes to get to Miami Beach. It should have taken us seven. We crept like crabs down Oistins Hill, winding our way from Yorkshire, where I lived at the time. You'd have thought we were travelling across parishes. We were only in Christ Church.

He parked in the shade along Enterprise road. He removed his glasses. For the first time, I noticed he didn't have on his swim trunks, like me, and would have to change. He wore long beige polyester pants, which seemed strange to me for many reasons.

I took off my glasses and stepped out of the car. Then I tossed back in my black tank top, and locked and closed the door. My cousin deftly slipped out of his pants and into his trunks, briefly bare-bottomed. He rolled his car keys into his towel. "Let's go," he said.

We chose the calm side of the beach. Had I been with my sister or even by myself, I would have dived into the rough side. Bigger waves, more action, a taste of danger. The stronger swimmer, my sister would have my back. Alone, I figured I could take care of myself — just don't venture out too far.

The point of this bath, however, wasn't to test my aquatic skills but to steep.

My cousin and I were only spending some time together. We rode the waves gently, with ease, like lilies on a pond, soaking up the sun. One hour, two maybe, we spent in the sea, occasionally commenting on the activities of the other bathers or the shape of the clouds or current events.

It was a quiet afternoon. There was little to nothing momentous about it.

Yet that afternoon is memorable to me for having been so peaceful, the type you wished and prayed there would be more of but knew there wouldn't be — at least not as many as you would like — because of age, routines, preoccupations.

We pulled ourselves from the sea, walked toward the car and toweled ourselves. We put dry clothes over wet and sat in the car. I put on my glasses, and my cousin did the same with his. Then we drove off — at a crawl — in search of something to eat before the sun set.

January 12

Comics in Barbados

COMICS ALWAYS HAVE been disposable literature in the West Indies. A generalization, this observation is probably less true of the French and Latin American countries, where art traditionally has had a greater political purpose.

The late Antonio Prohias, for instance, who created the long-running, wonderfully warped, Cold-War *Mad* cartoon, *Spy vs. Spy*, was born, raised and trained in Havana, Cuba.

But I remember a college friend once telling me about how his father had *Detective Comics* #27 when he was a boy growing up in Trinidad. They would read comics today and throw them away tomorrow, his father said.

It was only when my college friend told his father how much the first appearance of The Bat-Man was worth today — approximately US$140,000 — that he became remorseful.

He wished he still had that comic, he said, but for financial rather than sentimental reasons. Creator Bob Kane, the legend of The Dark Knight and that atmospheric, 1940's pulp-fiction funk meant little to him.

When I moved to Barbados, there were a couple of comic book stores in Bridgetown. One was very North American, located in City Centre Mall, with all the latest titles bagged and lined along a long wall. It had no name I can recall.

Another, Komik Kraze, was more modest, an upstairs establishment located just off Swan Street.

Two years later, only Komik Kraze remains, though moved out of town onto Lower Bay Street.

I don't know where Barbadians go to get their comic books. After 20 years as an aficionado, I still get mine from Montreal; a fellow collector makes sure my list is filled each month and holds the books until I return for a visit.

I don't know, either, if Barbadians particularly care whether or not they have a comics specialty shop. My eight-year-old brother-in-law can't read comic books and doesn't seem to mind in the least. He finds the word balloons confusing: "Which one do you read first?" he asks.

At his age, such things were not a mystery to me. But I grew up in a comic-book culture: my eldest brother collected comics, my school friends bought comics, we all read comics in class during reading period. My brother-in-law likes the pictures, though, and thinks Batman is cool.

I haven't been totally honest. Despite the high prices, say, $10 for a US$1.95 book, Barbadians can, and some do, purchase comics off the stands in certain supermarkets and book stores. The selection is neither wide nor current, but at least some very basic titles are available: *Iron Man*, *JLA*, *Wonder Woman*.

Maybe the absence of comic books in Barbados or elsewhere in the Caribbean makes little or no difference to anyone. There are those who will say it's no big deal if Barbados never produces a major cartoonist or comics creator who chronicles the glories and miseries of living on this little island in words and pictures. So what if Barbados never has a Captain Barbados, a national super-hero that fancifully embodies their myths and dreams and ideals?

To my mind, the most obvious loss is that a whole world of imagining is closed to a whole people. I'm not a fan of everything — sword and sorcery or science fiction novels aren't my first choice when I pick up a book — but I value the alternative perspectives, on art and life, reading a good piece of work in either of these genres affords me.

March 23

Prince of tides

THE MOMENT HE calls for cou-cou, you know he has been here before, is a regular. It's morning; lunch isn't for another hour and a half. But the waitress working behind the bar informs him the cook was preparing some "in case he passed by."

The cornmeal-and-okra delicacy isn't ready yet. He studies the menu, considers his options. He consults his wife. They decide on the Big Bajan Breakfast.

Austin Clarke ("Tom" to friends) reaches for an ashtray and lights up a Cartier. Dressed in white slacks, a tropical blue shirt and dark, round shades, he looks like a man on holiday.

"It has become a favourite," he says of the establishment, Pebbles Beach Bar & Restaurant, located on Graves End Beach on the outskirts of Bridgetown. The sound of the surf is soothing. "This is the beach I used to come to when growing up."

Instead of a *rendez-vous* at the University of the West Indies' Cave Hill campus, where he and his partner, Rosamaria Plevano, a translator, have been staying, we come here so she can swim while we talk.

Clarke orders a coffee; ignoring the three sachets of sugar on the side, he drinks it black.

"But I never went in too often because I can't swim, you see," he says, getting back to the sea. "I would have to steal away from my mother."

At 64, still a son of the soil even though he has spent almost 45 years in Toronto, Ontario, Clarke knows something about time and tide.

The title of his latest book is *The Origin of Waves*. It is the story of two Barbadians, John and Tim, once close childhood friends, who meet by chance in a Toronto snowstorm at Christmastime and spend an evening in a bar catching up on the last 50 years of each other's life.

Praised as Clarke's finest novel, it recently won the Rogers Communications Fiction Prize. "The last time I was here was in '94, during the elections," he says. He was working hard for the Democratic Labour Party then. "I'm here, I would say, on a vacation, really, although I came to do a lecture ["Nation, Language, and Literature"]. So there's less anxiety than the last. And this is the first time I've felt like a tourist, because normally I would be staying with friends."

Be this as it may, the success of *The Origin of Waves* no doubt has contributed to his laid-back attitude.

"It's a good feeling that this book has done so well. I didn't expect it." Actually, Clarke put aside *The Polished Hoe*, another book he had started but stalled on, to write this one. After working for the past few years as a member of the Immigration and Refugee Board in his adopted city, *The Origin of Waves* became an effort to prove to himself he still has what it takes to write a good book.

"All I wanted was to have the book accepted for publication," he says. "I really thought it would be a preparation for the other book."

The Origin of Waves is now in its fourth printing. For the first time in his writing career, Clarke has been sent on a promotional tour by his publishers, McClelland & Stewart.

As a result of all the attention, one of his memoirs, *Growing Up Stupid Under the Union Jack* (1980), and his

Toronto Trilogy, *The Meeting Point* (1967), *Storm of Fortune* (1973) and *The Bigger Light* (1975), will be re-issued this July.

Some critics have called the themes Clarke embraces in *The Origin of Waves* more "universal" than in those books. He has his own theory as to why his first novel in ten years has had such an enthusiastic reception.

"Most of my previous books, I think, have been mis-understood. My previous books dealt with Barbadians in Canada." This, he explains, makes his work political. Unfortunately, people also assume he only treats issues of race and not the human condition.

"I think the difference," he continues, "is that this book does not at all deal with that [political aspect]. So that the reader then has to relax and accept what the book is deal-ing with, which is simply very close friendship, nostalgia, and personal, I suppose, and psychological frustration."

Clarke is grateful for his good fortune — not that he takes it for granted. As the late Canadian novelist Robertson Davies once suggested, writing doesn't get any easier with age; the most a long-time practitioner can hope for is a greater understanding of what he or she has been doing throughout the years.

"You still have to question the usefulness of time spent writing. You have still to wonder whether the point you are making is a worthwhile point," Clarke adds. "You have to consider the fashion and the trends in writing."

At this junction, breakfast is served: a huge, white plate of fried eggs, bakes, plantain, fishcakes, flying fish, watermelon, tomato, and cucumber.

"It's been a long time since I had a traditional Bajan breakfast," says Clarke, pushing his plate toward

Rosamaria, entreating her to eat. She nibbles on the fruit then heads for the beach. Moving along, talk turns to the work of other writers. When asked about successors, he straightens up in his seat.

Clarke's air is professorial. He doesn't really talk to you, rather at you, but never above or down to you. His shades only heighten the impression.

"I'll give you two positions. One is the position of these writers who feel that they will overtake me," he says. "That's fine, if they're going to write better work than me…. I assure them that I will be writing when I die. The second position is my own. I consider them to be competitors, and I've told them so."

Clarke admits to tensions among black writers in Canada. "You really are writing for glory, if you can call it that — attention. But there's enough attention available that all of us can get a little bit." He has deep respect for Barbadian-born journalist Cecil Foster and the poet Dionne Brand, formerly of Trinidad.

If there is something that bothers him in Canada — more precisely, in Toronto — it is the current habit of East Indian writers from the region to segregate themselves. He insists Trinidadian writer Sam Selvon, a friend and mentor who spent the last years of his life in Calgary, Alberta, would never have considered himself anything other than West Indian or Canadian, and not, say, an Indo-Caribbean who happened to be living in Canada.

Regarding his own peccadilloes, however, Clarke is cagey. To him, character is fate and his forte. Consequently, traditional plotting remains somewhat elusive.

Clarke breaks to point out the sea. Rosamaria has swum out farther than makes him comfortable. I ask if she knows that old Bajan proverb about the sea having no back door. He nods gravely. "But, being Italian, she doesn't listen," he says.

He comes back to the conversation. "Of course, I cannot admit to having any weaknesses. I may not admit to having any strengths."

Clarke, quite simply, is fascinated with language, what it can do. The raves for *The Origin of Waves* aside, his personal best is *The Meeting Point*. His story collection *When He Was Free and Young and He Used to Wear Silks* (1971) ranks as favourite.

Upcoming is *Breadfruit 'n' Pigtails*, a book on "ways of cooking" — the "real" stories behind recipes like bakes — balls of fried batter my Mom calls "Bajan pancakes"— that was inspired by the social commentary columns he wrote in dialect for the *Nation* newspaper in Barbados. It is to be published by Random House Canada in January next year.

Following that will be more novels. Already finished is *The Question*, which is "essentially about the way words are used by men and women to communicate."

It may sound arrogant, but Clarke believes he has yet to receive his due. "No," he says unequivocally. His reasoning has less to do with ego than with necessity. "To say that means you may as well stop writing." And that, obviously, is something he is not at all prepared to do.

April 19

Welcome to Fantasy Island

THE WOMEN DANCE ON the bar, beer bottles at their feet. The air about them is smoky, sweaty. My companion, whom I'll call NB, is confused at the set-up.

NB was expecting a stage; there's little room for one. And a sit-down place this is not. Makeshift benches line a wall.

It's all a bit improvised. The men at the bar are laughing, shouting, stupefied. People spill onto the sidewalk, liming, hanging, hustling.

The sign in the entrance says you have to be 21 and up to enter. And that's where we are — in Bridgetown's lone strip club.

After an *Investigator* story on the Baxter's Road club and a *Nation* report on how three of its dancers were charged with lewdness recently, not to mention Evangelical reverend Lucille Baird's petition against vulgarity in Barbadian society, I've become curious.

I'm here to see for myself how lewd 'lewd' is, although I already know something about the topic. Montreal, the city about which Charles Dickens once said you couldn't throw a stone without breaking a church window, is also known for its strip clubs.

21 And Up is dark. NB and I stand at the back. It's hard to talk over the music.

"She doesn't look into it," NB says about the woman dancing.

"Uh-huh," I agree, amazed the patrons are allowed to touch her.

But the women don't take it all off. Two dancers in

red lingerie come on, do their thing. When done, two more in white lace appear.

"The other girls were more popular," NB observes.

One of the ladies in white, sweet-faced, is strikingly disdainful.

"She looks young." NB again. "I mean *young*."

She and her partner just go through the motions. The ladies in red were more enthusiastic.

And that's when the analogy hits me: This is *Fantasy Island*.

You know: that 1970's television show in which Mr Rourke (Ricardo Montalban) helped people live out their fantasies. "Smiles, everyone. *Smiles!*"

Even if you could ask why the disdainful lady in white was here (out of desperation, perhaps?), you couldn't forget the setting. The ladies in red were engaging, slapping away rude hands, flashing for money, flirting.

Of course, they were vulgar — winding your waist in strangers' faces and letting yourself be fondled for a few dollars by them are rough ways to make a living. The point is, here, in this place, they had to be vulgar.

The ladies in red played their parts with a smile, because to do otherwise would be to ruin the fantasy for everyone, including themselves. One guy at the end of the bar seemed to attract the dancers, and he tipped them generously when they enticed him.

Strip clubs are remarkable equalizers. The men here tonight are no different from the men who come on other nights, nor from the men who frequent such establishments in Canada, England, the US, Trinidad, black or white, Indian or Chinese. Neither are the women. The men come to catch a piece of tail, to hoot, holler, get hard, to drink, brag, behave rude. The women are here to make money off the excess testosterone.

I'd rather be dead than a prude. Life's too short to waste cultivating silly hang-ups. Still, strip clubs are not my fantasy.

Not counting 21 And Up, I've been only to two in my life, in Montreal: once for a high-school friend's 18th birthday then, the second time, for another friend's 21st. Each visit, these guys and I were surprised and disappointed the experience wasn't more stimulating.

Then again, I have fantasies I consider legitimate that I suspect others might view as perverse.

I see nothing in the club that is so wild as to send me past the doorman into an alley retching. Not this night.

By North American standards, 21 And Up is not so tame. I wouldn't expect what I see here to be played out on any street corner. I wouldn't want it to be.

But certain choices are meant to be personal, not public. And the purpose of all fantasy is the enjoyment — or endurance — of a scenario for its own sake.

May 25

Blessed assurance

SOMETHING WONDERFUL, though not unanticipated, happened to me this month: I turned 30.

Birthdays, to me, are peerless occasions for joy and celebration. How could the day you were born be anything but special?

This particular birthday, however, was a milestone year. Turning 30, like turning seven, 10, 13, 18, 21, or 25, is one of those lifetime achievements that is best described as a rite of passage.

It is a time when one moves truly from foolish youth into mature adulthood. At least, it is supposed to be.

At 18, I had much to learn about life, as I still do now I am 30. I expect this to remain the case when I am 40, 50, 60, 70 — until the very day I die.

For my 30th birthday, I had a wish list. It consisted of nine items and, with no small thanks to The Mrs, was completely fulfilled. At the top of my list, though, was to watch the sun rise, which I did through rainy clouds.

I received cards, phone calls and e-mail from family and friends, and was dined by The Mrs for breakfast, lunch, and dinner (at which point I was also wined). It was a day of expectations met, it was a day of genuine surprises.

But the day would have been badly begun without saluting the sun.

Since my days as a newspaper delivery boy, when my route had to be done before most people were up or off to work in Montreal, I've had a fascination with sunrises. Movie people call the early twilight, anywhere between four and five a.m., "magic hour." If you're up at that time walking the streets, watching them slowly come to light in a blue and yellow mist that softens everything it touches, you appreciate how apt the description is.

More than witnessing this, I just wanted to know I've lived to see another day, to know I'm alive in the Moment, happy for that grace if nothing else.

Listen: I've watched bullfighting in Mexico and gone moose-watching in New England, traveled through Europe, North America, the Caribbean, and been inspired by these regions. I've known passionate love, the kind so beautiful, so raw, it could almost be described as sacred *and* profane. I've met many interesting people, some famous, some not. And I've done work I'm proud of, learned to play the piano and the trombone.

But it ain't over, that much should go without saying. I don't know when I will die, but I do believe the best is yet to come, and that to live each day in this faith and fear, is to shine. I still feel like a big kid with plenty to experience in this world.

So what more could I have asked for, really, even on this birthday, except the continued blessing of life?

June 29

The Jews of Barbados

THERE IS A STRANGE, solitary feeling to the graveyard that leads the way to the Nidhe Israel Synagogue, like a whisper in the woods. More than bodies are buried here, but shards of Barbados' past. The broken gravestones, engraved in Portuguese, Spanish, Hebrew, Latin, and English, attest to this. The history of a people, a nation, is here, in the soil.

"Jews are known to have been present in Barbados since 1634," says Jimmy Altman. Sephardic Jews, they were from Spain or Portugal and had fled the inquisitions in their countries to Brazil, then under Dutch rule. According to *A-Z of Barbadian Heritage* written by Henry Fraser, Sean Carrington, Addinton Forde, and John Gilmore: "When Portugal reclaimed [Brazil], there were strong links between Barbados and the Dutch, and Jews who fled from Recife to Amsterdam received permission from Oliver Cromwell to settle in Barbados." *A-Z* cites the arrival of the first Jewish residents as being six years earlier than the date Altman offers. The first major settlement was not formed until 1654.

Fraser *et al* continue:

By 1679, there were 300 Jews in Barbados, and by the following century 800, and five burial grounds. The first Jewish Synagogue was built between 1654 and 1664 [in Bridgetown], and public worship was allowed by 1654, three years ahead of London. According to contemporary testimony, the Jewish community was charitable and pious, a model of the "sanctity of family life."

The Montefiore Fountain between the synagogue (whose name means "the scattered people of Israel") and the public library stands in honour of their virtue. As for the synagogue itself, it was destroyed in a hurricane in 1831, rebuilt in 1833, and sold virtually for parts in 1929. Its brass chandeliers were purchased by the Dupont Winterthur Museum in Delaware whereas other artifacts found their way into the Barbados Museum.

The neo-Gothic building wasn't resurrected until 1987, when Altman's cousin, Paul, a prominent land developer, other members of the Jewish community, and Jewish associations abroad raised the money to raise the roof again.

Altman moves from the cash register to the long counter at the back of the store, where he cuts cloth for his clients with a joke and a smile, always quick and courteous. He invites me to sit behind the counter.

He is the owner of this souvenir-and-dry-goods store. Established by his father, Altman's has been in business since 1956.

"I have been made to understand that those Jews from Brazil introduced sugar to Barbados," says Altman. Again, Fraser *et al* say "the exact details of when sugar cane was introduced to Barbados are not clear."

What is known for certain is that the present community of Jews is Ashkenazic, originating from central and eastern Europe, and it started with the arrival of his grandfather, Moses Altman, in 1931.

"My grandfather was on a freighter [from Poland] going to South America, and the freighter happened to stop in Barbados, and he got off at the docks and he liked it…and stayed on," says Altman while seeing to his customers.

Friends come into the store along with the regulars.

They talk about other friends, their families, business, gossip. Dressed in blue Bermuda shorts, a Polo-style shirt, running shoes, and white socks, Altman is breezy looking.

"There are about 20 families total in the Barbados Jewish community," he says, coming back to me. "You're looking at about 55 individuals."

Even with deaths and departures, these numbers have remained stable over the years. "There is a minor problem," Altman admits, "because when a community does not continue to increase its numbers, it does feel the loss of those who have gone on, and this puts pressure on the remaining members to try and keep things alive.

"With the offshore market expanding in Barbados, we have had new Jewish families coming in. But they're not here on a permanent basis."

As far as Altman is aware, the Jewish community does not reside in any particular area.

"They live anywhere they can afford," he says, noting where he lives, Christ Church, and the west coast. He would consider this a sign of their degree of integration into Barbadian society.

"I believe they've adjusted very well, because they're still here. I'm a living witness. I'm third-generation."

As I listen and take notes, a lady asks me if I work here. I tell her no and direct her to the man in the blue Bermudas. Then another woman asks me to measure the length of her skirt anyway.

"I'll be with you in a moment," Altman shouts. It's something he often repeats to me during our interview.

"There are many Barbadians today in our society who, somewhere down the line, have Jewish ancestry," he continues. Common surnames like Mayers, DaCostas and Barrow are Jewish in origin. "I don't believe we've ever felt any form of anti-Semitism in Barbados."

Altman, who is 49, recalls growing up in Hart's Gap, Hastings, as just another white boy in the neighbourhood. It might have had something to do with Barbadians' legendary religious tolerance or the low number of Jews in the island, but good relations with the community at large were and have been generally the norm. When his grandfather got off the ship, he did not speak English. He felt comfortable because the people here were friendly.

Altman can relate: "I'm a people's person. I love people."

Since their second coming, Jews in Barbados have made their contribution to the country's political and economic development. Aaron Truss served as minister of tourism in Tom Adam's administration (1976-1985). Israeli consul general Bernard Gilbert is firmly ensconced here. The community has introduced various forms of manufacturing, such as knitting mills, and opened a number of retail businesses.

If their members have encountered any problem other than small numbers, it has been the absence of a rabbi.

"A rabbi is a necessity in any congregation, because the rabbi will enhance the religious aspect of the Jewish people," says Altman.

"You know, when the original Jews came to Barbados in the '30s and '40s and '50s, all of those older members could officiate in the synagogue. They could do everything. And at that time we had no need for a rabbi, because those members were well-trained from back in the Old Country.... But today, because a lot of the younger members have not had that extensive Jewish education, you have to bring in an official rabbi for the Jewish new year and to perform weddings and so on."

The community manages — as it always has. Back in the early days, Altman's grandfather's home doubled as a synagogue for the Sabbath. (Before the restoration of the Bridgetown synagogue, a more modest synagogue, Shaare Tzedek, was built on Rockley New Road in Christ Church. It is used from April 15 to December 15.) And various members of the community, such as himself, are capable of conducting services on the Sabbath, which is observed every Friday.

On the wall behind the cash register is a picture of Altman's father and another of Altman's two sons, but that of his father, smiling smartly yet humbly in sepia, is clearly from a different era, even another world, and stands out.

Although well-traveled, Altman has never been to Poland, the land of his forefathers. Nor is he in any particular hurry to visit. "Maybe now that the European world has opened its doors to the western world, it will be more interesting for me now to visit."

The lull we are enjoying slowly dissipates as more customers, tourists, come in the store. They greet him familiarly. They've been here before. "From a religious aspect, I'd have to say I'm Jewish," Altman says to me before turning to them. "As an individual, I'm a Barbadian."

July 5

Scent of an island

EVERY CARIBBEAN ISLAND has its own fragrance. In Grenada, the scent is leafy. In St. Lucia, it is tinged with sulfur. In Barbados, the air is especially salty.

In Martinique, it is a mixture of oil and spice.

Smells link us to people as much as to the time and place those people inhabit. Being able to smell a people is a quality to be cultivated not only in politics or beer halls but also in travel.

It is a particularly useful skill to the weekend tourist seeking to connect with his milieu in a short space of time.

Although a taxi man could tell by The Mrs' physique and mine that we were *Antillais*, there is a vibe to the French Caribbean (as there is to the Spanish and Dutch) that is distinct from that of the English-speaking islands.

Martinique (425 square miles, population 359 500) is a curious mixture of the Gaulish and the African. You're just as likely to bump into a person walking down the street breaking a baguette as you are to spot another feasting on a big Creole dish of rice and fish topped with steamed plantain.

But, in general, Martinicans are a trim people. If there is an art to wearing close-fitting clothing, the women have it stylishly mastered. They seem to take their fine features for granted, unaffectedly. For their part, the men seem humourous and genuinely helpful.

At least in Fort-de-France, the costly capital carved into a mountainside. Full of narrow alleys and winding stairways, inviting danger as well as discovery, it is a city that begs exploring.

Communication can be a bother if not familiar with

French. People are a little surprised when you don't speak the language or are unilingual, although Martinique only recently introduced teaching English as a second language in its schools.

Places that can boast bilingualism as one of their national characteristics don't know how fortunate they are (like my ever linguistically divided Quebec). The benefits are so obvious.

A Dutch family, for instance — based in France but mobile due to the father's work in the oil industry — opted to take a tour with us in English of the long-standing Fort Saint-Louis naval base by *La Savane*. For them, *peu importe la différence*.

Also worth visiting are *Bibliothèque Schoeler* and *Cathédrale Saint-Louis*, both of which look like they were erected out of cast iron. Made from metal and stone, they were built to withstand even the most devastating *cyclone*.

Baie des Flamands, guarded by Fort Saint-Louis, is ever calm. Ferries cross it daily to the other shore, Les Trois-Ilets. During the week, motorcycles and minibuses race the highways and streets. You can hear them coming, whether from La Gallaria, the largest shopping center in the West Indies, or Saint-Pierre, the island's first capital, which was destroyed by the eruption of Montagne Pelée in 1902.

Still, the shops close for an hour or more on Saturday afternoons, and everything virtually shuts down on Sunday in one of France's most pleasant and sophisticated *départements*.

August 10

A time for peace

HE SHOUTED AT me the way I always tell people to — loud and hard, like a bark.

"ROBERT! ROBERT!"

When I walk beneath burning skies, my head is usually down and my mind focused on one thing: the destination.

He was standing in front of Cave Shepherd.

"Hey!" I ducked across Broad Street to greet him.

"I see you're hustling down de road," he said, extending a hand.

"I'm just trying to get in to work," I said, taking it.

"I see, I see."

"Last time I saw you, you had wheels." He honked me a few weeks back as he was driving past Pelican Village. I was coming from eating my lunch by the waterside.

"I'm waiting for a ride," he said.

It was odd to see him on foot. "Wheels," though a common term, was really an expression I picked up from him and used only when speaking to him about his car. He looked slightly ill at ease — exposed — and regretfully dependent.

Actually, it was odd standing on a street corner talking to him at all. A couple years ago, we had a falling out that resulted in him asking me to leave his house and me going very willingly. Of course, the dispute no longer struck me as terribly offensive.

My family has a fairly diplomatic disposition. When our tempers flare, however, they can scorch the earth. I've been known to go nuclear.

It's not something I'm proud of — it is something I

can control — but we, my brothers and sister, supposedly inherited our mother's sense of outrage.

That said, it takes a rather serious offence — a broken commitment, an act of reckless stupidity, bold-faced ignorance, outright prejudice — to set us off.

The quality of our conflict was such that, although an old friend of the family, I never thought this man nor I would ever have much of anything to say to each other again. The few, necessary conversations we had after the incident were hesitant.

But there is a time for peace and a time for anger. Clearly, we had gravitated back into each other's orbit despite our own inclinations.

I had to wonder if we would have gotten away from each other the way we did if Dad were well. This man was an old friend. Our family stayed at his house when we visited Barbados. For a time, he looked after one of my Mom's properties here, her Mama's house.

Dad, it was assumed, would have mediated. This man had respect and admiration for my father. Or would Dad have said it was my call, favouring neutrality over a potential conflict with his youngest son?

It's one of those questions I worry when making decisions that might go against Dad's worldview. How would he have counseled me? Would I have listened? The situation — would it have turned out very differently? Dad wasn't one to stand for foolishness. Neither as teacher nor as man. Had he been able to intervene — had he been well — more than the course of one forgettable dispute would be altered in my life.

It's remarkable, the animosities we foster only to let go. We may swear up and down to cut off someone with whom we've had a disagreement. Problem is we are rarely

100 percent sure if we can or should keep the oath, nor is time our ally in the decision-making process.

Some might say the human heart is as soft as the head, that's why. Not me; not quite. Look at the intensity and tenacity of the differences between people in Northern Ireland, the Balkans, parts of Africa, Guyana. Right or wrong, they thrive, virulently. Also, there are certain offences that are unpardonable.

It is not necessarily easier to forgive and forget, to seek reconciliation; simply, in some instances, it is inevitable.

"So how's work?" I asked. "Still getting some picks?" Again, I was using a language borrowed from him.

He shrugged, meaning not bad. "And you?"

"O.K.."

"The old man's in hospital."

I looked at him. "Nothing serious?"

"He's under observation. But he'll be all right."

We talked until we both had to move on, not for long, but long enough. And when I rushed off, head bent on the road, I was surprised, amazed: that we had so much to say to each other yet also at the possibility that we might, another day, have more.

August 17

The dog days

"THE DOG DAYS of summer" is something of a misnomer when applied to the end of August in Barbados. For summer is as much illusory as it is perpetual here.

Think of it: summer — in a place where it is almost always hot, where a picnic can be had any day of the week, any time of the day, where you can get a snow cone year round?

Summer, as it is referred to in the Caribbean (much like references to winter, spring, and fall), seems to me the creation of tourist boards and Utopians seeking adult playgrounds or paradises while conveniently forgetting why humans were thrown out of them to begin with: Eden can hardly exist with us in it.

So Barbados is neither playground nor paradise, and we generally talk of two seasons — the rainy and the dry.

Dog days nonetheless exist. They usually are felt around this time of year — just before back-to-school.

You can actually see their effect in the eyes of children still on the lookout for the ultimate holiday high — the experience that distinguishes their vacation, their whole year. They know: there are things to do before there's no longer all the time in the world to do them.

After a relatively dozy Crop Over, we'll all shortly be dealing with the budget, independence celebrations, Christmas shopping, pre-election campaigning, the year 1999....

So the blood flows differently because nature and her inhabitants now move differently, the rhythm of life seems to hurry up, in that last, frantic lap toward the end of the year.

The horizon, I've noticed lately, has been hazy, near-obliterated, for long stretches in the afternoon and early evening.

But when it's clear it's brilliant, glinting off a rolling sea free of heat waves or hurricanes.

I've noticed the slack-jawed expressions of people on the streets, walking to and fro, staring dreamily.

These people look just like the children, wondering: "My, the summer (such as it is) went fast. What did I do for the summer?"

And that's how they must feel, taken back as much as taken aback.

It doesn't matter that they're not children, that they've left their awkward adolescence far behind them and haven't seen the inside of a classroom in years.

They find themselves studying the matter.

But they're also thinking: of ways, perhaps, to take one last drive with the kids down the East Coast, to have one last moonlight picnic with family and friends, to go on a long bicycle ride through the country, or to orchestrate that romantic afternoon encounter — before the day the school bells ring again.

They are thinking, and they are waiting for their chance: to do exactly what they long to do — no worry, no rush — before being harassed, hounded, by changes in temperature and temperament.

August 31

Blame it on the rain

HAVE YOU EVER watched the rain fall?

Back in university, I took a course in Caribbean literature. The authors under review included Jean Rhys, V.S. Naipaul, V.S. Reid, and Edgar Mittelholzer. Out of the books we were required to read, those by Naipaul and Mittelholzer stayed with me most.

Naipaul's story about a man trying to find a place for himself in the world, *A House for Mr. Biswas*, impressed me with its scope and humour. In the other novel of his we did, *The Mystic Masseur*, also comic, the transformation of the eponymous East Indian into a true Brit seemed to prophesy the Trinidadian author's eventual entrenchment in England.

There was, however, little that was funny about Mittelholzer's *Corentyne Thunder*. A slim book, it was nervy, moody, elemental. The knowledge that its author committed suicide by setting himself on fire added to the gloomy allure of this novel about peasant life in his native Guyana.

Mittelholzer's observation of weather systems in *Corentyne Thunder* is over-the-top yet weirdly brilliant in how it conveys the emotions of the characters and propels the action.

Mittelholzer's death seemed unaccountable. Scanning his photo on the back cover, the blurbs and bio, I understood he must have been a troubled man, a neurotic, an awkward fit in life — yet a suicide?

Lately, I've been reading *A Morning at the Office*, which was passed on to me by a colleague. It's Mittelholzer's second novel.

Having worked at a number of odd jobs at various levels in society, Mittelholzer was not only familiar with the hopes and dreams of peasants. His description of a pre-computerized office in Trinidad (although the setting could be Everyoffice) is very similar in temperament and operation to today's high-tech ones.

A more or less typical scene involving a character's reflections on work: "Except for dictating a very occasional letter to Miss Henery, signing cheques, and consulting with Mr. Jagabir or Mr. Reynolds on some matter concerning the accounts — some matter which Mr. Jagabir or Mr. Reynolds would already have attended to with their customary efficiency, hence which needed hardly any attention from the Chief Accountant — Mr. Murrain had virtually no work to do (though upon him rested the responsibility of the accounting department). But realizing that it would be bad policy to appear idle, he had recourse to invent various subterfuges."

Of course, incidental attention is paid to how humans mirror nature (and vice versa): "Mr. Jagabir smiled as he regarded the paper. But like a patch of blue sky vanishing just as it has given promise of fine weather, the smile faded and a look of gloom and regret overspread his features."

I ask you again: Have you ever really watched the rain fall?

Watching the rain on and off the last few days has called to mind all these thoughts and more, unexpectedly: a remembrance of school days, melancholy laughter, clouds of thunder, and the best laid plans aborted — each memory unfolding into another. And I'm grateful for the memories — for the act of remembering — especially here and now.

Is this how it works, how thoughts come and go? Can I bottle the effect, patent the process, then dispense the elixir, free as hope? It has occurred to me, when watching Dad, that the only way to survive not remembering is to completely forget.

Besides running from it, cursing it, praying for it, what effect does the rain have on you?

I'm more of a cloud man; I find an overcast sky comforting, like a woollen blanket. Rain is like a wet blanket.

Still, there's drama in the heavens: days when the sky looks war-like, days it is peaceful, and days it causes the mind to drift.

October 19

Around Barbados in a day

HOW FOOLISH ARE boys as men, once weaned on the myths of their fathers.

Last Wednesday, I tried to prove at least one thing these elders told me about Barbados was as they remembered it. As a child, I listened to stories told in Montreal basements as if around a tamarind tree, stories by Dad and his brothers about our Bajan forebears — who they were, where they came from but, most of all, what they did.

"Do you remember...?" one would begin.

"He was the one...," another continued.

"That's right, that's right...," they all agreed.

So I rented a bicycle with the intention of riding around the island in a day. According to their legend, Barbados is small enough to do it, following the coast.

The Mrs didn't fully understand why I would do this. Neither did I. But my quest had to do with finding something good amid the violent crime, racial divide, and cultural compromise of the present day — something just as true when I arrived here two years ago as it was in my parents' day and would be when I left.

"To have hope, you've got to have love in your heart," I've heard it said. Well, I love my elders. But relationships are more than a function of love; they're about trust. There are some things we must confirm for ourselves.

10:24 a.m.: Started in Hastings, Christ Church, at 10:10. Making good time through St. Michael. Never thought I would feel comfortable riding a bicycle in Barbados: narrow roads, few sidewalks, fewer bicycle paths, reckless drivers. The sturdiness of the mountain bike helps.

11:00 a.m.: Find myself outracing the rain. That old thrill of challenging nature, accepting the impossible mission, makes me smile and speed up.

The upscale construction in St. James indulges my North American sensibilities. But the Bajan in me says, "If this is the New Barbados, we're in trouble." The glam hotels and posh pads aren't about renewal as much as slapping a veneer of sophistication over coats of vulgarity. We live, to borrow from Mark Twain, in a "gilded age," forgetting all that glitters is not gold.

11:43 a.m.: Stop briefly for rain and peanuts. Clouds are moving in from the west. As a kid, I used to ride my bike like a cowboy. Remember this going past a graveyard, which triggers thoughts of *Tombstone*, the movie.

12:03 p.m.: Walk into St. Lucy. Leg cramps caused me to dismount. The village of Six Men's Bay, one of Dad's old haunts, lies ahead. Look to my right, the east — it's raining where I'm heading.

(Expletive deleted.)

I saddle up.

12:29 p.m.: Take refuge at St. Lucy's Parish Church, a sprawling, stony structure. Shell peanuts while I wait for the rain to hold up, wondering (again) why I'm on this quest. *Crazy Canuck*, I curse myself.

A couple of workers are having a brawling conversation about "today's yute" and recent murders among them — as if people, young or otherwise, ask for the bad things that happen to them. I think to say this but don't, unsure of the difference it would make.

1:26 p.m.: The open spaces in St. Lucy remind me of lovely green places in the American north-east, and west.

I make it as far as the middle of Duncan O'Neal Highway, at a junction, before the wind and rain get heavy.

Despite my umbrella and cap, I'm almost soaked. I've got a choice: go on to the East Coast or retreat through Speightstown.

The clouds ahead are thick and dark; behind, they're clearing, lightening.

(Expletive deleted.)

I decide to abort the mission.

4:31 p.m.: Have returned the bike. Theoretically, I've proven the elders right: made it halfway around Barbados with time to spare, even though my quest didn't turn out as gloriously as I would have liked.

October 26

Christmas too soon

YOU'VE HEARD OF the Ghosts of Christmas Past, Present and Future. But do you know the Ghost of Christmas Too Soon?

Of course, you do. He, like a gate-crasher, is the spirit that descends upon the land before we're ready to "feel" or "look" like Christmas.

Officially, there are 52 shopping days left to Christmas.

To certain segments of society, particularly Barbadian retailers, this might seem a reasonable time to start promoting the season.

In Canada, consumers' wallets are fair game after Halloween, October 31. In America, you can start stuffing the Yuletide turkey any time after Thanksgiving, the fourth Thursday in November, if you like.

Independence, November 30, used to be the date to race in Barbados.

Within the last three weeks, however, I've seen Christmas commercials from Gillette and Harris Paints on the Caribbean Broadcasting Corporation's Channel 8.

There are rules in life: like "drink no wine before its time," "think before you speak" and "don't talk with your mouth full." Not only do they help us get through each struggle of a day, they promote better living.

Another rule should be it's bad form to show Christmas commercials, complete with tree and music, over two months before Christmas.

This may sound terribly arbitrary, even curmudgeonly. I like Christmas music; some of the best music I've sung is Christmas music. I like pines; trees are our friends.

But to everything a season.

The fact is you're just as likely to kill an occurrence by jump-starting it than by waiting for it to emerge gradually, naturally, as you get close to the time of its happening.

Think in terms of romance thwarted by an over-eager lover, and you'll begin to appreciate where I'm coming from.

The lights are low, you've just finished a fine meal with that equally special someone. Now retired to the couch, you sip wine, make small talk and occasional eye contact.

Then — Bang! — you toss the wine, lip-lock your date and completely blow the evening.

All this because you forgot one elementary truth: consummation is rarely as great as temptation. Or put another way: the beauty of the thing depends on the build-up, baby.

The benefits of being subtle are multiple, as are those of knowing when to take the controls and when to enjoy the ride.

People like to be eased into a mood, finessed, seduced, if you will.

There are reasons — some practical, some sentimental — the period leading up to the Holidays is often more exciting than the Holidays themselves.

So, believe me, I'm no Scrooge. Christmas is indeed the most wonderful time of the year. Peace on Earth and good will to all should be a credo we strive to live year-round instead of six or seven weeks out of 52.

Pipe in the Muzak. Deck the halls. Wrap those presents twice. And bring on the feast. I can't wait for Santa to come to town.

It's just all the early-in-advance hype I can do without.

November 2

The best of times

NOT EVERYBODY FANCIES lists. Some find them elitist, others call them limiting. They are rarely comprehensive, often focusing on the top 10, 20, 40, 50, 100, etc. And they can become outdated overnight.

The closer we get to the millennium, the more we might expect. The fact that lists aren't known to age gracefully has never really affected people's fascination with them. Fascination, after all, has as much to do with repulsion as attraction.

Lists are about priorities. They're about what we have done (check — give yourself a pat on the back) and about what we have left undone (scratch that — next item).

The following are personal lists of the 10 best and worst things about Barbados — in no particular order. They have taken nearly a year to compile.

The occasion of Barbados' 32nd year of independence seems as good a time as any to consider these lists — at a time of celebration, reflection, and, sometimes, transformation.

You may call the following a list of fame and a list of shame. But every country has its good side, its bad side, its ugly side.

Collectively, they form what is called national character, which is not who we pretend to be to the world at large, rather who we seek to be to each other on our own little island.

The 10 Best Things About Barbados

1. BICO ice cream — exotic flavours, great taste, it can hold its own against the likes of Ben & Jerry's or Haagen-Dazs.
2. Christmas corsages — a sprig of cheer that is a lovely holiday innovation.
3. The clouds — majestic, expansive, romantic, inspiring.
4. The beaches — their sexiness is not at all overrated.
5. Nicknames — comical and cute, more than anything else they are endearing.
6. Mr. Tee's Donuts — again, Dunkin' Donuts and Tim Hortons beware.
7. Decorated roundabouts — a bright way to light up the highway.
8. Sunday lunches — peas and rice, macaroni pie, baked chicken, coleslaw, fried fish, tossed salad, potato salad, ham, sweet potato, mixed vegetables....
9. Fresh fish — and an excellent variety, too.
10. Moonlight walks on the beach — see 4.

The 10 Worst Things About Barbados

1. Men who urinate anywhere — a nasty habit.
2. ZR conductors who try to stuff four people in a three-seat space — regardless their size.
3. Bajan arrogance — sorry, but God is not a Bajan.
4. Women who don't smile — an anomaly among a reputedly 'friendly' people.
5. Men who smile too much — out of lechery, not happiness.
6. A reverence for the mediocre — low standards are no standards.
7. Litter — whether personal droppings or public dumping.
8. Environmentally harmful expansion — you can't eat concrete.
9. CBC Television — see 6.
10. Over-the-counter service — not always the sweetest or the speediest.

November 30

Just being neighbourly

WE STOOD ON opposite sides of the guard-wall, men assessing damage. A tractor had ploughed into the corner bordering our properties, leaving the wall chipped and cracked.

"I spoke to the driver," my neighbour said.

"What did he say?" I said.

"Well, it's his tractor what did it. He would have to fix it, ain't it?"

I nodded gravely, looking down at the wall. My neighbour looked down, too.

He had repainted it earlier in the year, both his side and mine. I remembered buying some of the paint, Turkish brown.

"Did he say when?"

"No," my neighbour said.

We hoped it would be soon. We were good neighbours, after all.

"Good fences make good neighbours," wrote the American poet Robert Frost. The line is from "Mending Wall":

> There where it is we do not need the wall:
> He is all pine and I am apple orchard.
> My apple trees will never get across,
> and eat the cones under his pines, I tell him.
> He only says, "Good fences make good neighbours."

The speaker of the poem doesn't agree with his neighbour. How can good fences — blatant obstacles — help people become closer?

It is possible to read the verse from the neighbour's

point of view. The poem also suggests we all need our space, and we all need to have that space respected.

It is this kind of respect that has been known to breed safe relations between people. Another old saying that reflects the philosophy: "Good accounts make good friends."

But these sentiments formed no part of the reason my neighbour and I hoped the repairs to the wall would be made soon.

Although the repairs concerned us both, we simply didn't want the other to worry about them. We were like the speaker of the poem: the wall was there, between our houses, dividing our lands, but not us:

> Why do they make good neighbours? Isn't it
> Where there are cows? But here there are no cows.
> Before I built a wall I'd ask to know
> What I was walling in or walling out,
> And to whom I was like to give offence....

You see, I don't mind his prickly daffodils poking through the spaces in the wall onto my property any more than he minds my ant-infested bread-and-cheese tree hanging over his. When either needs trimming, we cut them regardless of where their roots lie.

A number of times, we've both hung over the wall, talking about gardening, renovating, his days in England before he and his wife returned to Barbados to retire, my yearning for Canada.

There may as well be no wall for all the tales, tips, fruits, and vegetables we've traded over and across it.

Just the other day, he was talking about bringing over

sorrel for me and The Mrs. We had some fresh from the store. Their leaves had spoiled, which he knew nothing about.

If he had been aware of this, he would have told us we should have known better in the first place than to buy any for the Holidays.

The last sorrel we had, and recently brewed, was also from him.

December 21

1999

Suffering the sun

To the world at large, the Caribbean has no worries. Apart from Jamaica (crime), Cuba (Communism), St. Vincent (drugs), Haiti (poverty), Guyana (political unrest), and one or two other unfortunates, the region is a paradise.

These are islands of perpetual sun, finely sanded beaches, all-inclusive resorts, and brightly smiling 'natives' (although the Caribs probably wiped out the Arawaks centuries ago, right?).

Island life — to an outside world fed by TV images of luaus (which are, incidentally, Hawaiian) and bred on the romance of Daniel Defoe's *Robinson Crusoe* — is the life. No one worries; we're all happy.

Isn't this the image we put across in tourism ads and other government declarations to Americans, Canadians, Germans, the Brits, even to fellow West Indians?

I've always resisted this portrayal of the Caribbean. Not because it is too good, too hopeful, for West Indians, or because there are other territories more deserving of the honour.

I resist this pre-packaged, in-the-can, say-no-more image of the Caribbean because it is as unfair as it is untrue.

This image of the Caribbean is damaging to a richer, reasonable, more comprehensive understanding of what these islands scattered between the Americas are really about.

I've been here and there around the world, listened to the travels of others and read the accounts of those who logged their journeys — and I have yet to discover paradise on Earth, especially where people are to be found living their everyday lives.

Still, I'm amazed at the reaction of otherwise worldly outsiders or visitors when apprised of the fact that we, too, are troubled by crime, drugs, AIDS, issues of sovereignty, imports and exports, the safety of our children at night. They act as if our tourist ads are lifted from our history books, and the sun is the ultimate panacea.

My dentist in Montreal had only this to say after I briefed him on current societal ills in Barbados recently: "Oh, well. As the French would say: '*La misère est moins pénible au soleil.*'"

His well-intentioned meaning: "If you've gotta suffer, baby, better it be in the sun."

He should talk to my colleague from Middle America. The subject of the sun often comes up with her.

After years of enjoying and enduring Barbados' flat heat, she has come to see the sun as "corrupting." That's her word for its effect: the sun can sap your strength, warp your senses, burn you out, make you go bad. Don't praise it until you've baked in it seven days a week, 52 weeks a year, she says.

Obviously, the Barbadian government's tourism campaign is to be commended. Last year, that industry pulled in $1.5 billion in revenue. Like the Caymans, St. Martin and Aruba, Barbados is to many one big tropical playground, which is fair enough — we can always use the money.

May as many Concordes as we can fit on the tarmac fly into Grantley Adams International Airport.

But let's not get too wrapped up in our own press. The money's good; it's just not the answer to everything — the same goes for the sun.

In broadly promoting the island as a playground, we forever run the risk of being viewed as children, hardly mature, inevitably dependent. We relegate ourselves to being a people whose concerns may be dismissed or ignored because they come from a land of sand, sea, and sun that, by our own admission, is outside real time and space.

January 25

After the storm

THE FIRST AND only hurricane I ever lived through was the Canadian Ice Storm of 1998.

For five days and nights last year in January, toward the end of my annual visit home, ice showered the island of Montreal. Freezing rain and snow encased roads, snapped power lines, broke the backs of trees, and shut down gas pumps.

In the beginning, the effect was terrifyingly beautiful. The world looked dipped in crystal. But as homes lost power, shelters became crowded and people started to die, many were only terrified.

The storm did not come with high-powered winds or crashing waves, yet the pains endured during that time were similar to those one would associate with the passing of a hurricane — which may be defined as "a storm of the most intense severity."

Montrealers, who, it was later reported, had been a fuse away from a total blackout, were still cleaning up in the spring and summer.

Last December, before the snows, I saw Montreal for the first time since the ice storm. Divided into suburb cities, one of its features is trees.

Tall oaks, poplars, pine, and maples, planted long before I was born or my parents bought a house there almost 40 years ago, towered over homes and parks, gardens and playgrounds.

These trees weren't for climbing; they were for admiring. They reached for the sky, and I ran beneath their sheltering limbs from one age to another, carelessly.

But the skyline was altered. The tops of pines had lost their spiked heads, and many maples had suffered amputations.

Proud oaks and famous poplars stood emaciated, cut down to size. The effect was unsettling.

Think of Barbados without its coconut trees or shak shaks or sandboxes.

Think of Jamaica without its mountains or valleys.

Think of Grenada without any spice.

Think of losing the everyday, the obvious, the comfortingly familiar.

Then close your eyes and feel the absence grow in your heart.

The damage to those trees was more disturbing to me than if city hall had been torn down and resurrected in the middle of the Saint Lawrence River.

Up to the day I returned to Barbados, I kept looking up and around, missing something.

I still do.

We take so much for granted: true love, kind people, good works, a warm bed. Most of all, we take nature for granted, its terrifying beauty but also its awesome grace: like grass filling a field, sea spilling onto sand, or trees crowding the sky.

February 15

Questioning the self

NICK WHITTLE IS into his first drink when I arrive at the Waterfront Café. Seated at a little round table under uncertain skies, he sips a lemon-coloured drink, coolly, overlooking The Careenage.

If ever slightly, his body language changes: as he catches me in his peripheral vision, his eyes shift. He sits up, extends a hand.

I feel like a Royal Canadian Mounted policeman of myth: they always catch their man. (The force's actual motto is "Maintain the right.")

One of Barbados' most progressive contemporary artists, Whittle is also among the more elusive of them. Despite his position as second vice president of the Barbados Arts Council, exhibitions at The Art Foundry, The Barbados Gallery of Art, and The Grande Salle, not to mention taking the Purchase Award in last July's Central Bank of Barbados Crop Over Fine Arts and Photography Exhibition, he has cited the fear of misrepresentation for his public reticence. His work, full of sexual tension and self-references, has not always been treated with understanding by the local press.

I'd been after him for almost a year.

Now, although his apprehension could hardly be called criminal, he seems resigned to an interrogation by a member of the same corps he has alternately courted and evaded.

"Looking back, as an artist who has left art school or university for 20-odd years, you realize the most exciting times were your years at university," he says, immediately putting our meeting in context.

Growing up in Birmingham, England, where he was born, Whittle calls himself "fortunate at the age of 11" to go to the Moseley Road School of Art there.

"Unlike most schools, its curriculum was biased in the arts. It actually fed a lot of the art-oriented businesses in Birmingham, the UK."

Many people encouraged him, not the least of whom were his parents. "[They] were liberal in the sense that they knew it was something I was interested in," he says.

Even though he knew he was 'creative,' Whittle wasn't sure if he wanted to be a painter, a filmmaker, or a photographer.

University was where he tested his talents and convictions. He worked "on a much larger scale: sculptures, relief." He tried his hand at various styles and techniques. And he met his wife, who would lead him to her island in 1979 and make it his, too.

"My work changed dramatically upon coming to Barbados," says Whittle. This was not so much in theme. His pieces became smaller without losing any of the "serial nature...diary nature" he had been exploring. Instead, Whittle found himself "intoxicated by the colour, the brightness of things," and a wealth of natural resources.

"Looking back on work I did in the early eighties, patterns emerge, the development of an iconography that is personally influenced by where one has been."

The sea, its shells, coral and sand — the whole Barbadian landscape is used in Whittle's work.

"I look at nature, and I see things that I can use to hopefully put across ideas that I have," he says plainly. "I think my work is full of a lot of self-questioning."

Whittle smiles slowly.

The 45-year-old artist is aware his queries aren't always welcomed or appreciated by Barbadians, even by those within the art community. He has left many a local critic and patron puzzled by his overt use of phallic (and vaginal) symbols in his paintings, the uncompromising mirror image they project.

When we look at nature, he observes, be it at a palm tree, a banana — whatever — there are sexual references. And that's because we put them there.

"We can't help but to see them," he says, emphasizing the whole process "is about identity."

Since he is a man, the references in his work are primarily to male genitalia. He is well aware Barbadians find this "disquieting." Part of the discomfort, he surmises, might be religious-based.

"But then there is this whole acceptance of double entendre in calypso. I don't know if it's a whole preconception of what the visual arts should be. But people have these ideas about what is 'good art.'"

He sounds frustrated and apologetic at the same time. Takes a sip of his drink. "I think it [my work] doesn't fall into any isms."

Whether or not this is strictly true, Whittle's work does relate to other work being done in the island. Among those with whom he feels an affinity are Karl Broodhagen, Stanley Greaves, Ras Akyem, Ras Ishi, Allison Thompson, and Lilian Sten-Nicholson.

If anything, Whittle's art is personal, representational, perhaps even spiritual in a confessional kind of way. Very much about the physical and psychological landscape of his adopted country, it is also being recognized.

"I think awards are important for artists to be seen as important members of society," he says of the Central Bank honour.

Grateful as he is, Whittle can't help being a bit disappointed in the money.

His top-place win earned him $4000. He notes that it is the same amount given to the person who comes in last in the Pic-O-De-Crop Finals for Crop Over. To him, this reflects on how Barbadian society values its visual artists and the work they do. Whittle looks up; so do I. It has finally begun to rain. We switch to a sheltered table. Closer to the entrance, we can hear the brassy wail of a sax on stage, the cacophony of kitchen clatter, and snippets of conversations.

"Opportunities for artists are only now being [realized] by government," he continues diplomatically. Whittle is further encouraged by the "tremendous" creativity demonstrated by students he has encountered at Queen's College, the secondary school where he teaches.

They seem to grasp art is a language, like English or Mathematics, that can and should be learned.

"Certainly, there is an unprecedented amount of activity," he says. In his estimation, artists are now more than ever striving for critical acclaim beyond Barbados' shores.

Last August's Caribbean Art Criticism Symposium, which he helped organize as a founding member of the Southern Caribbean chapter of the International Art Critics Association (AICA), was a manifestation of this desire.

"It was the first of its kind. It offered the opportunity for both artists and critics to come together and discuss issues."

He is already planning the next one, but what he sees

as being of even greater use to Barbadians is a national gallery of art. He welcomes last year's formation of a committee to study its feasibility.

"I think the benefits have not been realized by those in authority," he says, earnest rather than critical, although he is that, too.

As a teacher, painter, arts advocate, father of two, and husband, he is sympathetic to "those in authority." He understands true achievements are a blend of time, money, patience, luck.

In bad times — "and there are bad times" — he gains sustenance from his fellow artists. In good times, he quietly rejoices, all the while remaining cautiously committed to his calling.

"It's very difficult to balance all the hats you wear," he says, especially in a little island like Barbados. "You have to be a juggler. In terms of my own work, I'm continually trying to do it."

February 21

Speaking in tongues

"CAN YOU SEE far?" he asked, approaching with a smile.

"I beg your pardon." I had been eating my lunch on the beach across the road from Pelican Village, where I usually do, overlooking the sea.

He pointed across the water.

"Can you see far?" he repeated. His accent sounded German; he was pointing at a big boat in the distance.

"The boat? Yes."

"Can you see what it says?"

I was puzzled at first then caught his meaning. I could see the characters that spelled the name of the boat, but not clearly.

"My brother on a boat," he explained; his brother was the captain of a boat that was to sail to Barbados, and he flew in from Germany to surprise him.

He continued looking out to sea, his hands to his eyes like makeshift binoculars, smiling with what I now interpreted to be pride.

There are times, no matter how old we are, we wish for things the way a child would: irrationally, instantly, magically, strangely.

At that moment, I wished I could speak German. And this was indeed a strange desire.

It was strange because although one of my sisters-in-law is German I've never felt this urgent need to learn the language. My sister-in-law speaks fluent English. When I first met her, I thought of learning her language. She said not to bother, since we got along fine as it was, and that German was difficult to master. Educated in French, I've had greater interest in learning Latin or Spanish anyway.

But just then, watching this visitor to the island searching the sea, I wished I knew his native tongue as well as my own.

There was the need to communicate with another, the need to help, and also the need to know: the German looked like he would say more about his journey, his brother, his obvious joy, if only he could be understood.

Dad's father had a saying: "Leave the foreign languages alone until you can read and write your own." He had a point. Remedial English is much needed in our society, and not just at the elementary or secondary level.

But my grandfather, an autodidact, could speak Spanish, Latin, a little Greek. Furthermore, he passed on his love of languages to his children. Dad studied Latin and French. An uncle knows Spanish, Italian and French. All of these languages were of use to them, especially in their travels.

There are those who will cry, "Where in Barbados will I speak another language? What's the point, when everyone here speaks English?" Sometimes, the benefits of a little learning are as imperceptible as they are inevitable.

The other morning, I overheard a pleasant exchange between a Bajan receptionist and a German woman at the Tom Adams Financial Centre. The woman paid the receptionist's hairdo a compliment in her language, and the receptionist thanked her in kind.

The receptionist responded with only a few words to the woman. Only a few words were necessary.

April 5

The Knights of Nothing

WE GREET EACH other romantically. Hardworking men come into the office to slay modern-day dragons, we salute each other.

"Morning, Sir Lyle."

"Greetings, Sir Robert."

"Hail, Sir Christopher."

A nod. "Sir Terry."

Yet we have no Round Table. Our swords are pens. Our shields are our telephones. In fact, most of us have not even a desk to call our own.

Raised on comic books, police shows, and action movies, we greet each other in this way partly in the spirit of adventure, as men do, partly as a lark, letting the boys in us out to play when the king or queen isn't begging our curtsey.

We are the Knights of Nothing, the Emperors of Air — at this time in our lives.

In discussions on the creation of a regional court of appeal, this island's probable evolution into a republic and, lately, the removal of the Admiral Nelson statue from Trafalgar Square, soon to be renamed National Heroes Square, other questions regarding our sense of sovereignty have come to mind.

One of these concerns this business of being knighted.

While contemplating recently an idea for a short story about the life and times of a successful Barbadian who suffers a crisis of faith (in God, his family, himself), I was faced with naming the man's honours. Without thinking,

I had him knighted — become a Sir. It was the highest honour I could think of for him as a great Barbadian man.

No indigenous honour came to mind. Why not troubles me.

I should state up front that I consider an honour an honour. Whether made a *chevalier* by France or given a medal by Americans, one is being recognized for a job brilliantly done, usually over the course of a lifetime, usually touching many lives beneficially. Most honourary titles, in other words, are hard-won and should be respected for what they represent.

What I can't figure, in this age of our independence, is how a knighthood from the Queen is still so highly prized, how the minor noble title of "Sir" before Tom, Dick, or Harry can be regarded with such a sense of awe, of privilege, of class even, above others in or of the land.

My question is simple: how do we make our nation's highest, indigenous, civilian honour — which, incidentally, is the Order of National Heroes — similarly inspiring to the citizenry upon mention?

If only the answer were as simple as renaming a square. The romance of Great Britain is as powerful elsewhere as it is here. We aren't the only people, for better or for worse, still enthralled by its myths and traditions.

Americans have long held a fascination with the English, whom they fought over 200 years ago for their independence. Oprah once did a show on the American obsession with English titles and, for the sufficiently monied, with acquiring them.

We seem to be in the process or re-evaluating how we view ourselves, our history, and our culture in terms of our heroes and the monuments we erect to them. What's more, we seem to be coming to the realization that what they stand for might just be what we have stood for all along.

But we might need to broaden the scope of the debate and look more, to paraphrase an old African proverb, at what our heroes answer to, not only at what they are called.

April 26

In search of mall life

I've been exploring Ray Bradbury's *Yestermorrow,* a collection of essays published by Capra Press eight years ago. I picked it up second-hand while in St. Louis visiting my brother. That was in 1992, from a cramped bookstore that resembled a library squeezed into somebody's bedroom.

Its subtitle — *Obvious Answers to Impossible Futures* — was what attracted me. Bradbury, who is known largely for his science fiction, is a forward-thinking man. He believes in human potential and the literature's ability to help point the way for us to realize it.

He writes in the essay "Science Fiction: Before Christ and After 2001":

Science fiction then is the fiction of revelations. Revelations in time, space, medicine, travel, and thought. It is the fiction of the moralist who shakes his hand at us and says: Behave or I pull the switch! It is the fiction of the writer-theologian who shows man the mirror image of God in himself and promises him a real and true heaven if he gets off his ape-hunkers and fires himself into a new Genesis-orbit around the Moon and then into the abyss dark.

Many of the essays in *Yestermorrow* deal with designs for future living. Architect John A. Jerde notes in his "Afterword" that, despite Bradbury's accomplishments as a novelist (among them *The Martian Chronicles* and *Fahrenheit 451),* "it should not be overlooked that his visions about urban design, place-making and planning are equally astounding."

His pet projects are malls. Perceiving them as latter-day bookstores, endless eateries and art galleries, movie theatres and game rooms, adventure salons and lounge areas.

"Thus, in a single evening," he explains in "The Great Electric Time Maze", "we have been lost — gladly, in a womb of restaurants, only to plunge ourselves into a wilderness of Space and Time, so as to emerge and wander a labyrinth of shops from 400 BC, 1066 AD, 1928 America, sixteenth-century Persia, Shogun Japan, and the year 3199 in the Impossible Future." Or back to present-day Barbados.

I took a stroll through the new Pelican Craft Centre the other day. It's not a mall per se. Although officially opened April 19, it is, as of this writing, unfinished.

But I tried something I'm sure Bradbury would've advised. I imagined it into completion.

In the flash of the sun, I saw a dance of sculptures in the square and people circling them admiringly. In the blink of an eye, it was evening, a breeze was blowing, and a band was playing for a seated crowd dressed, as we say, in elegantly casual attire.

There is, it seems, only one café. But, surrounded by flowers and trees, the center may be a place for all manner of exchange.

I see schoolchildren running through the ironwork arches, eager for this show or that, a tired yet satisfied teacher being dragged behind them. From planes and boats, on feet and by car, travelers stream through the cream-coloured buildings, curious, excited, rewarded by their journey.

In the shade, young men and women lunch or make romance upon an afternoon. Later, older men and women come without fear to visit in the twilight.

This is not the way the center is now. Workmen's tools lie tucked in dusty corners. Most shops are uninhabited, uninhabitable. But it could be this vital. Walking away, I am still dreaming as I look back. Setting my sights ahead, nodding, I know we can make it so.

May 10

World of wonder

WE LIVE IN A world of contradictions. I understand, and then I don't understand.

Pick up a paper, lime on the corner, e-mail friends abroad — then consider the times, anytime.

The mind boggles at the signs.

Nelson now stands in Heroes Square. NATO bombs Kosovo for peace. *"Si vous voulez la paix, préparez la guerre,"* say the French. You want peace — *fight it out!*

And did you know that flying fish, half our national dish — such a sweet fish — is a scavenger?

Knowledge is good—and sometimes scary. I can't explain it.

The upcoming rainy season will be drier than usual. The dry season has been often wet.

We dump on the green while preaching land preservation and pollute the sea while promoting our beaches.

Bathers are warned not to venture into the Hot Pot, yet children swim in that stirring spot of sea by day, and lovers take each other there by night.

Why do we always do the things we know we shouldn't do? We live in a world of wonder, of amazement, of kerfuffle.

The Transport Board pays a foreign consultant "about $180 000" to tell them what they and everybody else in the land already know — that their management is poor to non-existent; off with as many upper-echelon heads as possible — only to see (have?) him chased back to England and his report scuttled.

People are being praised — rewarded — for doing

good jobs they either haven't done or can't do; no one minds; no one cares.

We revel in our limitations instead of seeking our strengths.

We want the best yet accept the worst — then wonder why nothing ever changes.

We want unity but can't come together.

What do we want? We are still blind to see the ones we hurt are you and me.

Girls becoming mothers before becoming women, men being boys and damn proud of it.

ZR workers say they get no respect, forgetting you can't get if you don't give — to passengers, drivers, pedestrians.

They've been calling Bill Gates the anti-Christ for some time now, but the man keeps growing richer and richer. Who are 'they'? The same people who keep buying his wares.

What's it all about? Everything jars, nothing pleases: just looking for someone to pin the blame button on.

Women get the vote in Kuwait, but can they choose their own mates?

Netanyahu stalls the Israeli-Palestinian peace process — "Impossible!" he says. Barak beats Netanyahu at the polls and declares: "There will be peace in the Middle East!"

Dr. Afrika calls condoms unsafe and expects grown men and women to take him seriously in this age of AIDS.

Everyone's a comedian when nothing's funny. Everyone's serious when they need a good laugh.

Why? Who knows? That's just the way it is and has been and always will be.

Right.
Sometimes.
Maybe.

May 24

Between men and women

IT WAS AN interview with a 19-year-old stripper, light evening reading. The Q & A was about her professional life and how — or perhaps why — she got into the business.

An older sister indoctrinated her, and the job had been paying for school and rent since she was about 17. She was single, on her own. Not that this negated the inevitable question about how her job affected her love life.

She said she wasn't big on foreplay but enjoyed oral sex. Further on, she described her first sexual experience. This explained her preferences.

All her subsequent experiences were re-enactments of that first time, which she remembered as beautiful and complete. She sought no greater satisfaction than what she had known at the age of 15 or 16.

But what had she been told to expect about that first time and by whom?

We tell our children to wait until they're 'ready' to have sex, but, in most cases, we don't tell them what to wait or be ready for.

This situation has puzzled me since I was a teenager. Now that my brother-in-law is on the brink of puberty, it tasks me.

I feel I will have failed him if I don't offer him some vision of the way things are, the way things ought to be, between men and women, as Dad did for me.

I want to save my brother-in-law from himself as much as from the world, telling him things like no hitting on another man's woman, whether she's with him or not. And hit a wall rather than a woman; better yet, strike nothing at all, walk away.

Then come back again after cooling off and talk about it. Say sorry and mean it when wrong. A strong man is strongest when all his strength isn't in his two hands.

Sometimes, a word or a look is all that's needed to reach another. Other times, though, only a touch will do. Reconcile instead of compromise so no one loses. But also know when to call it quits.

It's not only important to know who you're sleeping with, know why. Act responsibly — respect yourself. Inherent in this practice is respect for others. Don't hurt someone if you can avoid it.

Be faithful; know that a man who breaks more promises than he keeps is not someone people will want to deal with in a meaningful way. There can be excitement and fulfillment in commitment.

Relationships take tremendous imagination. Take nothing for granted. Build partnerships — share the load. Learn from a woman, especially if she is a good woman.

No matter how much you know, never believe you know it all. Listen to family and friends about their passions. Whatever the material, the source of inspiration, take it all in. Then put into practice the best of it.

Maintain an openness of spirit. Don't be limited by the narrowness of others. Read poetry — write it if you can. And cook with heart. Feel as well as think. Develop a sense of style and substance. Work at refining it.

Give pleasure but get it, too. Don't just make others happy — *be* happy. There are many, many things about relationships no one understands or ever will.

Yet it is possible to know what you want from a mate, and, once you do, to go after those qualities without regret. Dare to love as you would dare to dream. Make the wait worth all the risk.

June 7

Restoring the king

THERE IS NO love lost between me and cricket. A Canadian — a Montrealer — born and bred, you would do better to entice me with hockey (note the absence of 'ice' before the word).

The Montreal Canadiens have won the Stanley Cup — the Holy Grail of the hockey world — over 30 times, more than any other team in the National Hockey League.

It is a pleasant myth of the country that before Canadians can walk, both boys and girls, we can skate.

Yet, being of Barbadian parentage, my upbringing was also very West Indian.

Cricket could not — in fact, did not — compete with hockey for my attention or affection. Still, it was more than peripheral to my existence as a first-generation Barbadian immigrant's son.

I was schooled in its lore: the Three W's — Worrell, Walcott, Weekes, the white attire, Gary Sobers, C.L.R. James, the endless analogies of the game to life.

If nothing else, I was taught respect for cricket, for its value to West Indians, as a realm in which we could not — would not — be ruled. It was 'the king of sports', and we, when at our best, were more royal than any monarchy.

So it distresses even me, whose education in the sport was rudimentary, to read reports of its demise, its inability to compete as it did in the past for the hearts and minds of the young.

When it comes to cricket, I am truly a humble onlooker. But if permitted a few observations from the sidelines, they would be these:

Stage more One-Day matches. There are those who will say cricket is not cricket if not played over the course of several days. But every sport must adapt to the audience of the day to survive and thrive. Easier to relate to and endure, One-Day matches might capture more young fans who like their sports more fast-paced.

Make bats more accessible. From what I've seen, it's not common for children to have their own actual bats. This seems to me foolish. Part of the reason soccer soars in Brazil, hockey is hot in Canada, and baseball is big in the United States is because balls, sticks and bats, respectively, are given to children as soon as they can hold them.

Involve more girls. Yes, it's amazing how fast boys become interested in a sport when girls think it's cool. But cricket is part of their heritage, too, and they should be encouraged to play, not just cheer.

Teach cricket in the classroom as well as on the field. From James to Selvon to Beckles, we need to use the impressive and entertaining literature at our disposal to help rejuvenate the sport. Statistics and newspaper articles are informative, but they can hardly covey the passion of it all — historically, politically, culturally — to the uninitiated.

Promote the stars of the sport with gusto. If I have had any serious interest in basketball, it was because of Michael Jordan. If I watch a car race, I think of Mario Andretti. Wayne Gretzky, to me, is synonymous with hockey, Pelé, with soccer. Once their talents merit it, we should treat all our sports greats as our gifts to the civilized world. And they, like true nobility, must be made to appreciate their duties, not just their privileges, in promoting and preserving the sport.

Then who knows? Before long, the king just may be restored to the throne.

June 14

Flashbacks and déjà vu

EVERY COUNTRY HAS its problems, its failures, its frankly undesirables. Barbados, one of a few floating pearls in the Caribbean Sea, is certainly no different.

But there are times you look out onto a country, see it for what it is beyond the people and their constructs, and you can almost forgive it its inequities.

The country could be yours or it could be someone else's, merely adopted. You could be overlooking the sea at midday from a high ridge or across the flattest field of dust from the seat of a bus.

Whatever your connection to the land, whatever your vantage, whatever the time of day, you can't help but find reason to celebrate what makes the land unique — like no other in the world — and worthy of its place of pride and affection in the hearts and minds of those who would live nowhere else, or who visit it again and again.

You find joy in everything you behold.

I've heard it said it's virtually impossible to walk down a busy street and not see something of note. Well, yes. It all depends on your interests. The busyness of the street itself may be a distraction to what's really going on.

If I've walked up and down Fontabelle street a dozen times — past the Lower Green bus stand and Cheapside Market and the General Post Office — I've done so a hundred and more, but only within the last couple of weeks have I been assaulted by the fruit of the vendors' labours. The soft, pungent, sticky-sweet scent of ripening soursop and mangoes have invaded my nostrils to fill my mouth.

And it is a comforting taste, a wholesome taste. It

reminds you of things old and good and true about where you are in the world, the particular street you're walking.

It's kind of like the sea in the early morning hours. The smell is raw, foamy, and rock-salty. But it's also pulling, as if the motion of the sea is to be found in all its various elements, felt by all our senses.

And it's pulling us toward something, a realization.

There's more to gather from the rain than water. There's the faint smell of smoke rising from the earth afterward. There are the transparent colours of the rainbow. There may even be a pot of gold.

Coming from visiting the in-laws in the country last Sunday, I saw the sun set baby pink and powder blue across the parish of St. John. The following morning, in Christ Church, it rose again, giving off the same hues, lighting up the verandah as I walked by the kitchen. It seemed to be echoing itself.

Flashbacks or *déjà vu?* Is the coming of Crop Over, its festive air, etherizing my atmosphere? Or is it summertime, such as it is here, with its intoxicating heat, hot rains and lemonade laziness?

There are times you honestly feel someone's trying to tell you something — feel it right through to your bones. That someone could be God, if you like, but it could just be the world around you telling you about itself after it has gotten your attention.

You've only been smart enough to listen and understand some of what it has to say.

June 21

Karl Broodhagen

KARL BROODHAGEN doesn't sound so good over the phone.

I make my pitch in my most cordial voice. He's going to be 90 soon (today, in fact), and the paper would like to do a piece on him for the occasion as one of Barbados' leading visual artists. I'm fairly straightforward; it's a fairly straightforward piece.

But I have to add more when I've already said enough and the line seems to go dead: about the meeting being at his convenience — if he doesn't mind.

"Well, I've not been well. My stomach has been giving me trouble."

He's tired, irritable. I can hear it in his voice.

"It doesn't have to be this week."

"No, we may as well do it sooner. I may not be around much longer."

Even getting directions to where Broodhagen lives on Strathclyde in Bridgetown turns a little testy. After giving me fairly detailed instructions (I am to look for a guard wall overflowing with allamandas), I ask the colour of the house.

"Don't worry about the colour of the house!" he snaps. "The colour of the house isn't important. You'll only confuse things."

As it turns out, the house is the same pale yellow as the allamandas and even has a name — Glenrosa. Broodhagen's wife of 59 years, Eunice, lets me in, retreating so suddenly I wonder if I've actually met her or only dreamt her.

Recalling the occasion of my visit, I'm indulgent. Turning 90 can be a troubling, unsettling milestone.

It's not every day a man turns four score and ten years. Some people mellow with age, taking, in the words of "The Desiderata," "kindly the counsel of the years, gracefully surrendering the things of youth."

Others tend to sour, ever aware there are more years behind them than ahead.

And some people just plain don't like birthdays.

Once Broodhagen and I are sitting face to face in the living room — there are busts and framed paintings and other *objets d'art* from a lifetime of creation everywhere — my first question is inevitable.

"So tell me, how does it feel to be turning 90?"

"Not so good," he says, stretching to open the window behind him. There's a light breeze, and the sun shines through the lemony curtains. He rubs his stomach, adjusts his belt. "Most people feel it is whatever it is. It has creeped up on me, so I never really realized it."

Broodhagen gets up from his chair, comes back with a piece of paper with writing on it. I notice he is barefoot. He sits back down.

He claims he has no plans for the day. "I don't like big celebrations. The school was thinking about something, but I wouldn't encourage them."

By "the school," he means Combermere, where he taught art from 1949 until his retirement in 1996. Actually, he started the art programme at the secondary institution, in the days of Major Noote, at the behest of two of Barbados' best known writers, George Lamming and Frank Collymore.

Broodhagen refers to the piece of paper in his hand, rattles off the names of former students: artist David

Gall, author Timothy Callender, architect Erskine Mapp. There are many who went on to do something with their creativity.

"That's my life," he says. "I've been tied up to that all my life."

Teaching art, more than practicing it, has been Broodhagen's main occupation. He admits he could not have made a living from art alone in Barbados. No matter how high-profile or lucrative, the occasional government commission can't compare to consistent government support of the arts. Even so, after all these years of being what he would describe as a "part-time" artist, he is still drawing and painting and sculpting with enthusiasm.

"This is what I do. I get all excited when I see nice figures and nice heads. One can never get tired."

BROODHAGEN COMES from a family of artists. An uncle in his native Guyana was a musician and painter. A cousin there has lived a life similar to his in its broad strokes, working as both teacher and painter. And Virgil, the second oldest of his three children, who all live in Canada, is a well-known painter in his own right.

Broodhagen immigrated to Barbados with his mother when he was 15, the son of Guyanese parents with French, Portuguese, and Dutch blood between them. His first job was as a tailor in Bridgetown.

Besides art, he taught "the science of boxing" at Combermere; though diminutive, he was swift and sure in his younger days. Yet it seems art has always been, as he says, "so much a part of me."

After decades of satisfying work, including *The Emancipation Statue* (Bussa) at the Haggatt Hall Roundabout and *The Sir Grantley Adams Statue* on the lawn of Government Headquarters, there isn't much he feels he hasn't done. "The only thing is to do more," he says.

In the next breath, Broodhagen confides there are three "heads" he would like to do. One is of T. S. Marryshow of Grenada. He has always admired the late regional federalist. As for the other two: "I don't care to say."

Broodhagen works from life, now and then from photos. He shows me a catalogue to an exhibition in which his art is currently appearing in Washington, D.C., called *Parallel Realities*.

It is clear "people and their personalities and their figures" remain his favourite subjects. Because of the limited time he always had in which to do his own thing, Broodhagen had to focus. "I have developed a very sound knowledge of what I do," he says bluntly.

The basis of that knowledge is a commitment to realism. He finds contemporary Barbadian art increasingly abstract. But he attributes this to greater exposure to outside influences.

"I never thought I could have an exhibition in Washington," he says. "I wouldn't say I'm satisfied, but I like and I'm encouraged by the progress that's been going on."

If there is anything he would ask young and not-so-young artists to remember as they move forward, it is the importance of drawing.

"If you're doing visual art, the fundamental is drawing," he insists, "and you can never do enough drawing.

As a matter of fact, the better draughtsman, in my opinion, is the better artist." Behind Broodhagen, the window is chattering. The lemony curtains whip up with a faint hint of rain. Looking around the portrait-plastered room, he again laments the government's lack of commitment to the arts.

He has a collection worthy of preservation; it has been suggested to him that officials would do well to acquire some of it, perhaps even start a national gallery with it. That would be a brave, new venture for them.

Broodhagen falls silent.

"I have not been much into talking in the past," he says, an odd remark for a teacher. He pauses briefly and smiles, recognizing he hasn't spoken quite the whole truth. "Of course, if you're talking art, that's a different story altogether."

July 4

The class of '99

"THE KIDS ARE all right. It's the grown-ups I'm worried about."

These are the closing words to an article I read on the evolution of rock music some years ago. I forget their precise context, but they came back to me last Wednesday during my brother-in-law's graduation from St. John's Primary School.

The adults led the show, which isn't to say we stole it. We did the necessary: offered remarks, presented a principal's report, requested the obligatory valedictory speech, and solicited a featured address.

We were predictably longwinded and terribly earnest, often speaking just above our children's heads: not *to* them, rather *at* them. But we tried, and they did their best not to be distracted and to understand where we were coming from.

It seems as if now, more than at any other time, we, meaning the older generations, have placed all our expectations on the young even while lamenting their failings. Not a few of the speakers made much of the fact these tender, brave hearts would never again be as good or innocent as they stood before us now.

They would be entering "the lion's pit" when they entered secondary school in a few months, wherever they are going. They might expect to be seduced by all manner of wickedness, from drugs to television, from violence to pornography.

I felt for the graduates. I don't remember being given such tough talks even when I left university.

The afternoon picked up when the children took the floor, so to speak, in old St. John's Anglican Church. They sang songs, recited poems, performed a skit, and danced for us. They did what children, it is said, do best: have fun.

We adults sang along and applauded. At some points — during the skit, *Dare to be Different,* about a boy choosing the right path over the wrong one and the blessings of a good mother — they had us cracking up.

Still, the mood was melancholy. Nodding and smiling with the others in the audience, I was focused on the eyes and actions of these little men and women, trying to interpret what they meant and what they might mean.

Some people often ask what the arts reveal to us that is practical, useful. In their performances of "Guantanemera" and "I Believe I Can Fly", there were signs of things to come not fully in evidence when the graduates were standing at attention or being presented with their awards of merit and excellence earlier that afternoon.

I saw the stressed out university grad and the drugged out high school drop-out. I saw the suicide victim and the murderer, gun in hand. I saw singers and dancers and actors and those among them who would suffer for their art or ideas or lifestyle.

I saw well-meaning fathers and no-nonsense business-women. I saw the next member of parliament and the struggling teenage mother.

I saw everything they might be play itself out in front of me.

Whether graduating from primary, secondary, college, or university, the class of '99 are not only the children of the next generation but of the next age. To paraphrase the

American writer Grace Paley, they will have to deal with the open-ended opportunity of life in these *fin de siècle* times.

July 5

Remembering Dad

There's a cool dampness in the air this morning, and I'm thinking about Dad again. It's the twilight month, August, approaching the last quarter of the year, when all we have done and left undone converges. I've been thinking about him often.

Dad would be preparing for school if he were still teaching. His subjects were history and geography, yet — trained in Barbados before completing his studies in Canada — he knew so much about everything. He's probably having breakfast right now with my Mom, his concerns far from the classroom. Or maybe not.

He's retired, has been since the mid-'80s, when he was diagnosed with Alzheimer's. Dad says little that's coherent these days, so you can never tell where his mind may be at.

Such persistent thoughts about my father can be scary. Being at a distance from him, I never know what to make of them. They come and go in a mystifying mist, for as long as they may, wrapping me in uncertainty.

Am I thinking so much about Dad because he is not doing so well, and I am in some way feeling his distress? He's in good hands — the best — my Mom's. Still....

Am I thinking so much about him because I feel a certain guilt from time to time about not being at home? For roughly four years before moving to Barbados, he was also part of my day-to-day responsibility. Now....

This may sound foolish to those who, as Saul Bellow would put it, believe there are no mysteries, only the unknowables.

Well, this much I know: Dad lives in me. While visiting one of Dad's older sisters in Brooklyn one autumn, I caught her watching me. We were sitting at the kitchen table, talking, eating. Before I could ask her what was wrong, she said, "You look and sound so much like your father." I have two older brothers. Out of the three of us, this is said about me the most.

So maybe I've been thinking about Dad so much because I'm doing for him what he can no longer do — keeping his memory alive. It's as if, the more I remember him, the more I remember *for* him.

Those who think a father — a man who would be a good father, I mean — is superfluous are dead wrong. One of my best friends from high school, who was raised by his widower father, always used to say he never missed having a mother — but that, he confessed, was because he didn't know what he was missing.

I find I'm still learning from Dad, as if he implanted me with a time-release capsule of knowledge and wisdom that would outlast him. Little observations he used to make about God, man, and nature strike me now as immense truths: "You've got to dialogue with people"; "That which is base can never be made honourable"; "We are only here for a time."

Am I thinking about Dad so much because I'm wondering — worrying — about how much of him *does* live in me? And....

Dad wasn't the perfect father. I remember my Mom once saying she felt he should spend more time with me, though I didn't see how he could have or why. He worked pretty much regular hours. We took summer vacations as a family. He wasn't the type of father who wouldn't take you with him to the bank or store or for a drive. He taught me the piano, tennis, how to swim....

But, yes, Dad had his faults. Even if it is his strengths I focus on rather than his limitations these days.

August 30

The man who broke the Trident

IN ANOTHER AGE, you would call Grantley Prescod a Renaissance man. Teacher, organist, artist, honoured public servant, the designer of the Barbadian flag — he has been all these things and more in his rather active 72 years.

The only problem is he is retired these days, happily. And he wouldn't quite take to the description as he doesn't see himself in that light. He has been of a curious turn of mind since he was a child.

"To tell the truth, I haven't looked at myself in the mirror for a long time," he says as we chat in Queen's Park, overlooking the cricket field. "I do a lot of research, a lot of reading. I've always been concerned with what's been happening next door, with how people live."

A girl passing with a baby, a fellow collecting soda bottles, a tamarind from the tree above our heads, which sheds little leaves like tossed confetti — these are all of great interest to Prescod, glasses perched on his nose, pen in top pocket.

This engagement with the world around him has much to do with the community of Mapp Hill, St. Michael, where he was born and still lives, and St. Barnabas, very much next door.

"I grew up in a district where there were all sorts of people: blacksmiths, tailors, carpenters, joiners.... It was interesting to communicate with these people, find out the sort of life they live."

"I think this is something which is not fashionable with the young. They don't care about their neighbour, how other people get along, and it's a pity."

Prescod cracks the tamarind with his left hand, eats it, spits out the seeds.

"You don't see many of these around," he observes, savouring the sharp sweetness of the tree's fruit.

Prescod knows something about the difference between the children of today and yesterday. He was an education officer in the Ministry of Education from 1977 to 1987. More notably, he has spent most of his life dedicated to teaching (he has never married) and still sees himself as an educator, even though the last time he addressed a class was in 1992.

"I've been teaching since the time I was 16. I taught the primary school and at secondary school. I taught at Erdiston College," he says, which is where he trained as a teacher.

Prescod also taught at the University of the West Indies, Cave Hill. His subjects were art education and education. He obtained his master's in art education from Temple University in Philadelphia, Pennsylvania, after attending Bristol University and the West of England College of Art in England.

"Right now, I'm doing all sorts of odd things around the house I haven't been able to do for a long time," he says, reiterating the pleasures of a leisurely life. He has more time to work on personal art projects and get out to choral recitals.

"I look forward to any kind of music. I'm a big fan of calypso…. Can take one or two reggae."

But it was Prescod's skill in art — and singular interest in coats of arms — that led him to design The Broken Trident in 1966, the year Barbados became independent from Britain.

"For many years, we used to have a crest," Prescod explains. "At one time, the Barbados Government issued a stamp with the crest of Barbados. There was Britannia, being pulled by sea horses," riding the waves, her trident in hand.

When Barbados gained independence from Britain, it was time not just for its own coat of arms but a flag. An islandwide contest was launched.

"And I was tossing it around, how to use this trident," says Prescod. "It was only the last design I had done.... I had done about 14 others."

The late Harold Connell, then curator of the Barbados Museum and on the panel of judges of the contest, was particularly impressed by the design — one of 1 029 received.

"It was one of the few flags that was technically correct," Prescod says modestly. "I [had done] a little bit of heraldry."

He was awarded a gold medal, a scroll, and two cash prizes for his effort.

Prescod opens his hands evidently.

"Well, the money is gone."

One was $500 donated by the Advocate Company Limited, publishers of Barbados' oldest daily newspaper; the other amount, from the government, he can't recall.

The scroll he had framed and now hangs in his living room: it was signed by Errol Barrow, Barbados' first prime minister, in recognition of Prescod's contribution to "our free and independent country."

"The first flags were printed at Parkinson's," Prescod notes casually, in fleeting thoughts of the secondary school where he himself taught drawing, painting and ceramics.

There was some uncertainty as to whether or

not Barrow would have a flag to fly November 30.

The chosen flag was supposed to be sent for approval to the Royal College of Arms in England, where it was also to be printed. Knowing Prescod was into silk screens, Barrow asked him if he could do the flags using the school's facilities if necessary.

Prescod did about six or seven "originals." Although the makers in England sent the official flags on time, some of his were presented to Cave Shepherd at the country's oldest department store, the Advocate and Barrow: he placed it in the Cabinet Office at Government Headquarters.

Of the five craftsmen of Barbados' symbols of independence (Lester Vaughan wrote the pledge of allegiance, Irving Burgie wrote the words to the national anthem, C. Van Roland Edwards composed the music to the anthem, and Neville Clarke Connell designed the coat of arms), Prescod is perhaps the least mentioned during this time of year.

He doesn't feel appreciation for his contribution to the institution of this country is "altogether not present," yet he would like to see those who make such contributions recognized sooner rather than later for them.

"This happens all the time," he says with a slight smile. "You live until a certain age an active life, then you retire — and you're not known." There are stories about Barbados, he insists, that the young and not-so-young should hear. Retired or not, Prescod is working hard to make sure the greatest of them are told.

November 28

Untamed hearts

Close to half of all local marriages are ending in divorce.

— *Sunday Sun* back-page lead story, November 14, 1999

Every relationship is an implicit war of philosophies; the stakes are the relationship itself. Only if one person wins, it's all over.

— Robert Cohen, "Between Hammers"

ONE OF THESE days, I'm going to write this book. I know I'm going to write it because I can feel it growing inside me like a rage.

This book is going to be about my generation and relationships; it's going to be about love. It's going to be about what we really want and about wanting what we really can't seem to get — at least not as we would like it.

I'm sure versions of this book have been written before, by other authors in ages past. And maybe my book will be awful, but I'll do my best to represent.

I look around me at the men and women of my generation, and I see the choices we've made and the lives we are building for ourselves, the setbacks we've known, and the pain we've suffered.

But regardless the successes or failures nothing seems right without someone to share all these things with, without that person to laugh at, complain to, brush your teeth beside, sleep with.

Nothing seems right or fair without a mate; forget all the cute terms and euphemisms we use to describe such an individual, to lessen our embarrassment at our need.

And I think I find this remarkable because we — my generation — came of age at a time when people, not just women, but men and children, were encouraged to be ultra-independent.

Who needs a man? Who needs a woman? Who needs children? Who needs parents?

Well, the age-old fact of the matter is we all need somebody, and why so many of us have tried so hard to convince ourselves otherwise is increasingly beyond me.

Pride, maybe. Fear, most likely. We're all just trying to cover our hearts, which seem too easily bruised by others who presumably don't think or feel as we do about the finer things in life.

Yeah, I can see all these reasons and more.

But maybe things would be better if we got over ourselves, let our guard down a little, and simply admitted that what I want is what you want, is what everybody, sane and not-so-sane, wants, when we want it. And that is to be loved for who we are.

Let's finally out with the truth for a change. Forget all the nonsense about being absolutely fine even when we're absolutely alone (which doesn't mean we're lonely, right?). We've had enough nonsense.

What we want, when we want it, is for somebody we like to see us as we see ourselves; accept that, respect that, love that as he or she would nothing else — which is to say preciously and endlessly — and then for that somebody to allow us to return the blessing.

But first we have to understand it's not the greatest sign of weakness, the most vulnerable position to be in, to admit this out loud to another, rather a sign of great strength, of the utmost courage and character, a position from which everything begins to appear most clear.

December 6

Sand for snow

WHAT REFLECTION IS to writing, love is to cooking: essential.

The smell of butter and essence, of raisins steeped in wine, of peppers and spices — these are some of the rich, sweet smells of a festive season to me.

But a recipe out of a cookbook does not make a meal special. Following instructions, even to the letter, does not make dough rise.

The fruits of life are food; their preparation should be handled not only with patience but with care. And every recipe tells a story, often about good times, holidays, celebrations, of places we have been or know.

Sand for snow. Gifts from overseas. Cards strung up from wall to wall, the prettiest, year-round. Afternoon strolls in Queen's Park decked out in your Sunday best, everyone wishing everyone, "Good day! Merry Christmas!"

For my Mom, this is the story her dark fruit cake tells, a Bajan specialty that she long ago translated for me. As a boy, the story always seemed otherworldly: No real snow for Christmas? All-year cards? Yet, at the same time, it made me yearn to see Christmas in Barbados. Though family and other commitments take me home for the Holidays, one of these days, I will.

The following recipes tell their own stories, too. The plain cake is about summer picnics to Long Sault and Carillon Park in Ontario, to Plattsburg Beach in New York. The banana bread is about how my older brother Pat found this recipe in this Caribbean cookbook, added his own fine touches to it then passed it on to me. These aren't Christmas stories, true. But when I bake, I bake to remember: love, family, laughter, peace. I bake to celebrate.

Mom's Plain Cake

Although similar to other types of 'puddings', this cake is lighter than a pound cake yet not as spongy as a yellow cake.

18 tbsps butter, softened
½ cup sugar
4 eggs
½ cup milk, or water
4 tsps vanilla essence
2 cups all-purpose flour
3 tsps double-acting baking powder

Cream the butter and sugar until the mixture is fluffy. Beat in the eggs thoroughly one at a time then stir in the milk (or water) and vanilla essence. Add the flour and baking powder. Continue beating until the batter is smooth.

Preheat the oven to 350 degrees F. Grease the cake pan with butter and dust with flour. Pour the batter into the pan and bake for one hour or until a thin knife inserted in the center of the cake comes out clean and the cake pulls away from the sides of the pan. Let cool. Serves a family, if only for a day.

Pat's Banana Bread

This is a light-coloured loaf whose combination of vanilla essence and nutmeg gives it an aromatic flavour.

2 large, ripe bananas, chopped
1 tsp vanilla essence
18 tbsps butter, softened
¼ cup sugar
2 cups all-purpose flour
1 tbsp double-acting baking powder
⅛ tsp salt
¼ tsp ground nutmeg, preferably freshly grated
¼ cup seedless raisins
1 egg

With the back of a fork, mash the bananas to a purée. Stir in the vanilla essence and set aside. Cream the butter and sugar until the mixture is fluffy and set aside. Combine the flour, baking powder, salt, nutmeg, raisins, and egg. Add to this the bananas and the butter mixtures. Stir the batter until it is blended and smooth.

Preheat the oven to 350 degrees F. Grease the loaf pan with butter and dust with flour. Ladle the batter into the pan and bake for one hour or until a thin knife inserted in the center of the loaf comes out clean and the loaf pulls away from the sides of the pan. Let cool. Serves same as above, maybe longer if you bake both.

December 13

2000

Donkey treks and nutmeg jelly

THE ECOTOURS ARE what catch her eye.

The hotel's brochure promises rafting down "magical Beau Sejour River," hiking up Mount St. Catharine, the island's largest mountain.

Grenada is known as 'The Isle of Spice' — there are more spices here per square mile than anywhere on the planet — but The Mrs is more intrigued by the donkey trekking than the nutmeg jelly we are served at breakfast.

Unfortunately, she doesn't have the necessary shoes. Even a morning spent searching literally up and down St. George's for some 'soft wares' proves futile.

What we find in the capital instead is Strongman.

"Hey, you guys take a tour of the island yet?" He's the van driver who brought us into town. Short, stout, and dreadlocked, he had called me back to his window to hand me his card. It read: "Strongman's Tours & Taxi Service. Island Tours — our specialty."

I kid you not.

Starting from our hotel in Grand Anse the next day, we cruise up the south-western side of the island toward Concord Falls.

Grenada, which celebrated 26 years of independence from the British February 7, has a number of waterfalls. Concord's are lovely. But Annandale Falls are the more impressive of the two we visit — not to mention free. Bathing is allowed in both.

Grenada is also known for long, crystalline Grand Anse Beach. Second to it would be Levera Beach, on the island's north-eastern tip. Basically unspoilt, it has a basin-like pool corralled off by a reef. From Lavera's rippling shores, Sugar Loaf, Green, and Sandy islands can be glimpsed through hazy sunlight.

Along the way, Strongman points out a radio station in the parish of St. John (there are six parishes in all) that was used as a military base during the 1983 "rescue mission" of Grenada by the United States following the murder of socialist prime minister Maurice Bishop.

Bishop was executed by dissidents within his own party. His New Jewel Movement was supposed to usher in a real age of independence and prosperity for all Grenadians. It was a failed experiment, ending in a bloody coup.

Many of the houses we pass in the mountains are little more than shacks on stilts, mounted that way as protection against hurricanes. There are people outside them, washing, talking, liming.

"Hard times," says Strongman soberly. What appears cheap to tourists, he informs us, like the cotton khakis I bought at the mall near the hotel, is expensive to the average Grenadian, because of low wages.

Still, at night, the houses look as if they are built in the sky, the greenery is so rich.

Before Grand Etang, we stop by Carib's Leap, which is a bit disappointing.

The site where Carib Indians leapt to their deaths in 1651 rather than surrender to French colonists, it is now just a sheer, 100-foot drop at the end of a parched cemetery in Sauteurs marked by a faded, hand-painted sign.

Grand Etang Lake is far more interesting. It's in what was once a volcano.

No one, it is said, knows exactly how deep the lake is. "It's true," swears Strongman.

Driving toward Grand Etang, he recounts a legend about a Chilean diver who came to sound its depths. He went down one day, but he never resurfaced. "No one ever saw him again," says Strongman, too seriously.

The lake could very well be bottomless. Grand Etang supplies all the southern part of the island with water.

Surrounded by a silent forest, though, it seems peaceful to The Mrs and me.

Green-rimmed by stocky reeds, the surface of the lake glistens with the rays of the setting sun.

February

Sand, sea, sun — and stars

"HOW MANY ARE you?" he says. "I can take ten." Curtis Moore stands by the door to the telescope room. The children count themselves as a couple of tourists and wait their turn; Moore tells them to watch their step as they enter. Both the children and the tourists are eager to look at the lights in the sky, up close.

Summer is a good time to see Scorpius and Saggitarius to the south. On a clear night, you can see the Milky Way, "billions of stars in the center of the galaxy." Now, they're viewing the stars of Alpha Centauri, which look like two red and green sparks through the 14-inch Celestron telescope.

When people talk about Barbados, they often talk about the sand, sea and sun. But they never talk about the stars. The ones in the sky, that is. Watching Moore with this large group of locals and tourists at the Harry Bayley Observatory, you can't help wonder why.

"We have tried to serve the school system by educating the children," says Moore, the president of the Barbados Astronomical Society, which runs the observatory. Sitting in the second-floor library, we can hear the impressive rumble of the telescope directly above us when it is rotated. "Every Friday night, weather permitting, we try to show patrons and visitors what is in the sky. Unfortunately, there are no planets in the sky now."

The Barbados Astronomical Society was co-founded in 1956 by Dr. Harry Bayley, a renowned Barbadian physician. Following his death two years later, the society decided to build an observatory in his memory. In 1963, on Clapham Hill in the parish of St. Michael, the observatory opened its doors to the public with a 12½–inch Newtonian Reflector telescope.

From the looks of the library, the observatory has seen better nights: the walls could do with a coat of paint, and the bric-a-brac furniture is less than conducive to study. Moore, who is in his 40s, admits the observatory — from the ground-floor lecture room to the third-floor telescope — can do with an "upgrade."

The Harry Bayley Observatory maintains its atraction as the only observatory in the eastern Caribbean. What's more, it has the best of both worlds, being perfectly positioned to see all of the northern sky and much of the southern one, too.

The society is a non-profit organization committed to the development of astronomy. Open from 8 p.m. Friday and 6 p.m. Saturday, the society charges visitors for a tour of the stars. Other than that, it depends on government subventions and private donations.

The society's goal is to be "a centre for science," not just an observatory. It helps Scouts and Brownies get their astronomy badges. When anything happens in the sky, it is "bombarded" with calls.

"Generally," says Moore, a civil servant by day, "Barbadians are developing a strong interest." This is especially true of the young, who are keen to explore the stars using their island as the launch pad.

Numbers vary per night. The society has had small groups of a half dozen people. Then there have been "situations where we've virtually had to shut down this place."

The conjunction of Venus and Jupiter February 23

last year (the planets were within 0.2 degrees of each other) attracted 400 people — all floors and surrounding grounds were full.

At the time, between the schools and the hotels, the society's marketing was noticeably aggressive. You could see more in the sky then. This year, cloudy nights have been a problem. "Astronomy has a weakness if you're viewing," Moore says: "the weather."

Another is urbanization. One of the problems with the observatory's location lately has been light pollution. It can diminish visibility as much as a full moon (because of refraction) or the haze caused by air pollution.

"Even here, on the perimeter, we saw more stars in the past years before businesses were here," Moore notes.

The best time for viewing is after 12 a.m., when the atmosphere is cooler, the level of air pollution is at its lowest, and lights start to go out. Those in people's homes, that is.

But the summer sky is a good sky for viewing. Between Scorpius and Saggitarius, there are plenty of nebulae — celestial bodies — in the Milky Way. From where Moore often stands, "You can't expect to get any better."

July 31

Facing the lion

And what is most significant, we seem to need very urgently to let others know about our paintings and carvings and landscapes and music and animals. We need desperately to communicate, a need which is at the heart of the human condition.

John Wickham, "Final Inscription"

IT'S NOT OFTEN you come face-to-face with a literary lion. This is especially true when your landscape is Barbados, where these great cats seem an endangered species.

When I first came to the *Nation* April 1, 1997, most of the staff were not expecting an associate literary editor. Even after a year of writing the Onlooker column for the Monday paper, many did not know my face.

On the heels of hasty introductions and a tour of the place, I bumped into John Wickham. It is fairly safe to say he was not expecting me either.

I knew of John as the *Nation*'s literary editor.

There was little more I knew about him at that time. I did not know he had been a senator and was still affectionately called so by his colleagues. I did not know he was the editor of *Bim*, the Caribbean's premier literary magazine, which gave writers like V. S. Naipaul, Jean Rhys, and Edgar Mittelholzer their first serious exposure.

I did not know he was the author of four books of stories and essays, the one published by Longman, *Discoveries*, still in print. No one had told me any of this: not my employers, who probably viewed these facts as common knowledge anyway, nor my Caribbean Literature professor at McGill, himself a Trinidadian. And John certainly never said anything during my period of probation.

That was so much like him. I had to discover his work outside of his column, People & Things, in visits to book stores and by querying him about what wasn't available there that I could get from his locker.

John Wickham died Tuesday, August 29, at the age of 77 on a beach, quietly. The qualifier is necessary. Although I believe everything happens pretty much for a reason, I can't help but think John's end was in keeping with his life.

Despite an attempt at an authorized autobiography (though flattered, he grew impatient with my questions and reluctant to elaborate, and then we found it hard to find time to meet), I can't pretend to have known John Wickham the man. I can't even claim to have known Wickham the writer.

John was, I often thought, self-effacing to a fault, personally and professionally. In discussing his passing with one colleague who knew him longer than I, she surmised he was the type of man who yearned for more recognition as a writer — and his last column, "Final Inscription," certainly bears witness to this assumption — only to find himself incapable, perhaps, of properly pursuing it.

JOHN SEEMED TO write simply for the love of it. Yet just as one should never marry only for love (or money), writing for passion alone can be damning.

This isn't to say John was a pushover. People often mistake composure for ease. There was much to John's character I sensed: generosity of spirit, integrity, a passion for excellence, humour, seriousness of purpose, gentility most of all. Ease, however, was not a word I associated with him.

John was too opinionated for that. He may not have

been the obvious firebrand his father, Clennell — that man with the fountain pen whose column John inherited — was in the *Herald*, yet as a Caribbean man he had no less definite views.

This I felt most strongly when I read "Notes From New York" in *Always Elsewhere*, an anthology of black travel writing that came out of Britain two years ago.

In this personal essay, which appeared in *Bim* in 1962, John writes about a visit to the Big Apple. "Set down, not against one's will, especially not against one's will, in any place," he begins, "one cannot hope to learn anything of the nature of the place or prevailing spirit of its people by asking direct questions." Then he goes on, somewhat in a heated rush, to describe his encounter with 1960s "New York, America," with a sharp eye.

WHAT MAKES "Notes" so memorable — apart from John's elegant, sometimes old-fashioned way of turning a phrase — is his observation of people, his awareness, in his attention to details about their appearance and surroundings and conversations, of who they are and what their lives must be like.

There is great humour in "Notes," and criticism and exasperation. ("Along the Jersey turnpike at sixty miles an hour and soon we were passing wide fields in which the corn was bustin' out all over. The broken down shacks in some of the fields brought the South to mind.") There is also great empathy for those struggling, humbly, to appear no less dignified than they are regardless their circumstances.

John, quietly yet proudly, showed me *Always Elsewhere* soon after he received his copy. I commissioned a review of the book for the paper then wrote one myself for another publication, largely because of the variety of writers in it. But another part of me wanted to champion his cause, to roar for the lion in a way he wouldn't.

I couldn't write enough either about his co-editorship with the poet John Stewart of *The Oxford Book of Caribbean Short Stories* last year. I saw it as a fitting cap to his literary career.

His column had ceased being fresh. He would never finish the only novel of which I heard him speak, *Prospect*, for he had no desire to. Health problems, including failing memory (particularly noticeable to me), were slowing him down, and trips to the office were less frequent. Writers don't so much retire as retreat when their wizardry with words, like lost magic, begins to fade.

Still, it is most difficult to champion a man who, despite a desire for more recognition for his work, paradoxically denied any interest in the literary limelight. At least in the time I knew him, the way he presented himself to me. Yes, it is the work that's most important; every writer must know this to write, and well. The other truth every writer must know in order to write, and excel, is that somebody gives a damn about what he is writing.

And many of us did, John.

September 3

Against time and tide

RACHEL MANLEY sits overlooking the sea at Hastings in Christ Church, squinting against the glare of the early setting sun. She sips her tea and talks. She sounds older than she is — she's had an active life, three marriages, two children, many homes — yet very solicitous, like a kindly Jamaican aunt.

Her small talk — about family, politics, beaches, the writing life — is anything but. In Barbados to promote her latest book, *Slipstream: A Daughter Remembers*, Manley seems like a woman who is now very much at ease with herself. Her brown hair is wispy free; her enquiring eyes roam, haunted and haunting. She apologises: "All Manleys are longwinded." But a more just statement is that they are genuinely gregarious and interested in people.

There's something wholly sympathetic about her. It may be her grief talking. Manley wasn't always so diplomatic.

How much of her character is indebted to her father, Michael Manley, is made clear in her carefully observed memoir about his life and, especially, death.

"— From grief," she confesses, slowly, almost solemnly. That's why she wrote the book. "The last few pages were written at my father's bedside while he was dying."

Manley, a published poet ("I fled to prose"), had always wanted to write about her family. She first wrote *Drumblair*, which won the 1997 Governor General's Award for Non-fiction in Canada, where she lives when away from Jamaica. That book was about her grandfather Pardi, Norman Manley, Jamaica's first premier and the architect of its 1962 independence, and about growing up in his house, from which the book takes its title.

Next, she would write about her grandmother Mardi, Edna Manley, arguably Jamaica's best known artist, who loved horses and mountains and wood. And, finally, she would deal with her father, who twice led Pardi's People's National Party to victory: in 1972, holding on to power for two terrific, turbulent terms, and again in 1989, at the age of 64.

But then her father was diagnosed with cancer.

Manley thought she would have more time. "Because, to me, Daddy was eternal," she recalls. But she didn't; he wasn't. Within three years, he had left politics; by 1997, not long after *Drumblair* came out, he was dead. His story urgently became the second book in her proposed trilogy.

"I think I wrote the book because I couldn't help it," she says. In other words, it would have been harder not to write it. Yet Manley is quick to add: "All books, for me, are difficult to write in that they're work."

The title of this one refers to the destructive currents created by two large engines: those would be her father's and her country's. For *Slipstream*, on another level, is the story of post-colonial Jamaica. Although, in Manley's opinion, her father "nearly but didn't destroy himself" in working against time and tide, he did succeed in destroying Jamaicans' inferiority complex. "Of all the Caribbean people, we are most definitely who we are, I think, defined," she says with bitter satisfaction.

Slipstream came out in Canada around the time of the death of Pierre Elliott Trudeau, one of the country's most daring prime ministers. Trudeau was friends with her father (and godfather, the late, great Barbadian prime minister Errol Barrow; Manley also lived and worked in Barbados at the Caribbean Broadcasting Corporation during the '80s). Like him, she says, her father gave his people a sense of themselves and their place in the world that was undeniable.

Then she makes an odd admission, particularly for a memoirist, or maybe she makes it because she is one: "I have a very bad memory for things that don't interest me, but when something catches my memory, I hold onto it."

Those times stuck. She has no doubt, for instance, the Caribbean would be "further along" if it had persevered with the West Indies Federation in which her father and grandfather believed. Nor does she question "that it is right and good," and inevitable.

Slipstream was actually a bigger book. There was more politics to it; her editor cut about 200 pages from the over 500-page manuscript. The excised material was researched rather than first-hand accounts. Manley's satisfied with what was left in. She still cries when she reads it and hopes readers aren't put off by any excess of sentiment.

"The emotion just throws you apart...there is no coherence to the universe when you have lost a father," she says. "But I hope it's forgivable, in the context of what he meant to me."

November 12

2002-2003

Coda

Coda: how or why

MY MOM CLEANED Dad's mouth with a Q-tip. After she shaved him, she washed his face and combed his hair. She then placed tissue under the straps of his oxygen mask. The straps were adjustable but cut into his cheeks. She was conscious of the lines they would leave.

Dad was diagnosed with Alzheimer's in the fall of 1984. He was 58, she was 50. For 18 years, Dad — teacher, traveller, sportsman, scholar — weakened and faded. Except for respite care and family assistance, my Mom looked after him, at home, for nearly all of those years.

Alzheimer's patients usually live five to eight years. Nursing-home placement is inevitable. Finally, Dad lay in a hospital bed, dying. Ever since I moved to Barbados, I had been coming home winters to be with him, never knowing when he might slip away.

That I was now present was a minor miracle. I was made redundant by the *Nation* in April and flew up in September when it looked like Dad wouldn't last the fall. Money was tight, Dad recovered as best he could. My Mom did not expect me to return so soon. But I had been coming every winter for the past six years (The Mrs hadn't spent a Christmas with her family since we married), and I wasn't about to stop. Not until Dad was dead.

There is no other way to put it. Every time I came up, it was in the expectation, the hope, that he would die. Sick almost 20 years, already at an advanced age: it could happen at any time; I wanted to be there. I could not, for all my life, remember him not ever being there for me. And I had spent enough time in the Caribbean to understand-how uncommon a trait that was for too many West Indian fathers. Dad was big on understanding. If you could understand a thing, he said, there was no need to fear it. So I was coming to bear witness.

There was reverence in My mom's ministry, too, the way her stiff hands massaged the hair grease into Dad's soft scalp, the delicacy with which she replaced the mask. Coming from a family of Anglican teachers, lawyers, healers, and writers, I didn't wonder why as much as how this could have happened, to him and to us. The way I handled Dad's illness was both stoical and casual. Dad never said he should be placed in a home if his situation became too difficult for the family to manage. What he said was "I'll be here until God's ready for me." He never specified where.

My Mom said she'd be there for him. There was also routine in her faithful touch. She and Dad immigrated to Canada from Barbados newly married in the late 1950s, during a time when you were what you did and proud of it. My Mom was a nurse, until the end.

Sometimes, less as time goes by, I wish Dad hadn't left the decision for his care up to us. It's possible he didn't have the presence of mind to give it much thought. Or that my Mom's presence negated such thoughts. Alzheimer's took him by surprise; for what it's worth, I've had time to reflect on the devastation it can cause. Whenever I forget something — something I thought I would always know — I often get upset with myself. There's this pressure to remember, to *not* forget, that can crush those closest to you.

Still, it is doubtful we would have wanted Dad anywhere else but home. He was wonderful to be around, tender and secure. As it was, his Alzheimer's was like an intense period of deprivation, like a premature mourning. Only in his utter absence am I starting to realize how unutterably persuasive his example was — *is*. Dad wasn't a saint, but he was a man it simply made sense to want to love and follow.

My Mom and I left the hospital at 7:30 that morning. Dad died an hour later, not long after we reached home.

Rachel Manley was right, you don't know how you'll miss a loved one, a parent especially, until he or she is gone, dead and buried. It made no difference that I hadn't had an actual conversation with Dad for almost 15 years. When he was alive, regardless how sad the situation, there was always a sense of hope for his reprieve. It has not been easy, missing him.

I knew there would be some void, an emptiness in the universe, a space stripped by his passing. I expected to be left howling in it, raging all the time, like an orphaned child. And I do feel this way most at odd times, when I'm reading the mail or studying what to cook for dinner. I could be alone or in a crowded house. I feel this when it's inconvenient, when the emotion threatens to pull me under or blow me apart, limb by limb.

But what I have learned about love, as a man, I have learned from Dad. Love is rarely convenient, nor is convenience a prerequisite to loving. More than anything else, these two lessons sum up the strength of his presence in my life.

Dad died January 3rd, 2002. I remember him daily.

No matter what happens — how or why — I pray I always will.

August 2002

Home, Back Home

THEY LEFT BARBADOS for Canada on domestic and farm labour programs, or as reward for service to the Crown during World War Two, or simply as stowaways and castaways. My Mom and Dad were among those daring, pioneering West Indians. Regardless their class of ticket or personal intent, the promise was of a better life — better jobs, better money, better opportunities. It was up to them—and their children — to make good on that promise. The journey was, for many, a dream come true.

Someday, they would return to their island: to retire, reminisce, die. A lifetime later, I have returned in my parents' place. The dream is in reverse, upended. 'Home' has become 'Back Home', that phrase often used to describe Barbados from a distance. 'Here' is now what 'there' used to be for me, but not quite.

Their immigrant's dream, that fable, was never my own. Nor was the dream romantics have in cold, damp countries of a warm, dry life. Whatever dreams I had in coming here, 'Back Home', have changed over the last several years.

How a place becomes real to us, given enough time and exposure... How we can grow forgiving of its tight borders (and all borders, regardless how expansive, are inevitably tight)... How its fields and hills and people overrun us, like clinging vines or conquering armies, despite our best defenses...

Before long, we're used to our new space. And we start to wonder: Is this what makes a house a home, a country our own?

At the same time, we can never deny, never shake that

haunting sensation, that where we've come from is where we'll always be. Its terrain shows on our souls, and we move with ease through its streets; it doesn't matter how long we've been away from them. Something greater than desire ties us by the proverbial umbilical cord to the land, and... our land. And we discover, as all explorers and colonizers and immigrants do, that there is no place, no space, no country, including the world we've left and the one we've come to where we can live, comfortable and whole.

Home or 'Back Home'? An accident of birth or a sleight of geography? We are neither fully here nor there, because we are never where we expected to be. Wherever we find ourselves, we must be.

December 2003

Robert Edison Sandiford is the author of *Winter, Spring, Summer, Fall: Stories, Attractive Forces* and *Stray Moonbeams*. His articles have appeared in *Caribbean Travel & Life, The Globe and Mail, The Gazette, The Comics Journal,* and *The Antigonish Review,* among other publications. From 1996 to 2001, he was a columnist and an editor at the *Nation* newspaper in Barbados.

AGMV Marquis

MEMBRE DE SCABRINI MEDIA

Québec, Canada
2003